MORE YESTERDAYS THAN TOMORROWS

Paying-It-Forward To a Time I Will Not See

HANK VAN PUTTEN JR.

Published 2023 by Your Book Angel

Printed in the United States
Edited by Keidi Keating
Layout by Rochelle Mensidor

ISBN: 979-8-9897121-0-6

ACKNOWLEDGEMENTS

First and foremost, I want to thank God for giving me the strength and intestinal fortitude to focus my mind and complete this memoir which has been a process for over thirty years.

I need to thank my parents, both of whom I lost before they had the opportunity to see in me the fruits of their efforts, and the evidence of the wisdom they passed on to me in the short time we were together.

To my wife Gail who has pushed and pushed and pushed me to "just sit down and finish" throughout our reconnection after being apart for over forty years. I love you more!

To our children, grandchildren and great-grandchild - unknowingly, you challenge me each day to be to best version of myself for each of you.

To my BF Kemp who has always been there when I needed him.

To the many mentors throughout my career who have traveled with me - Frank Rife, Jon Saphier, Jeff Howard, Bessie Lyman, Sam Turner, Al Fortune, Wanda Speede, Irwin Blumer, Jeff Young, Matt King, Carolyn Wyatt, Beverly Tatum, Peggy McIntosh, Lee MunWah, Murph Shapiro, Manuel Fernandez, Carroll Blake, Bunny Meyer - THANK-YOU for touching my heart and being both a guidance a guardrail during our moments together.

To my PJI family who have been allies on this pathway to justice and taught me to trust the process - Rachel Allen, Lauri Lott, Shari Koopman, Jen Danilowski, Liana McGowan, Michele Lima, Celine Kavelic, Kari Whaley, Stanton Reed, Aida Diaz, Rudy Darden, Maria Georgio, Mollie McLaughlin.

To Keidi Keating who has been a lighthouse for me throughout this publication process. I appreciate your honesty, professionalism and the human connection you bring to our conversations across time zones.

INTRODUCTION

In today's interpretation, moving the goal post is considered problematic. However, that is exactly what Hank Van Putten has been doing his entire life. It started with his desire to become a crossing guard, a dream, as it turns out deferred. At the time, he saw this as a great disappointment, a failure on his part. From that day on, he continued to set higher goals, systematically and methodically moving the goal post on a regular basis to achieve success.

This book chronicles his earliest memories of his experiences in school, church and family. It provides a detailed commentary of how this young, black determined boy became a leader in the field of education and DEI work, that continues to this very day.

From the very beginning, Hank displayed his love of learning, sometimes being almost too smart for his own good. Often excelling in his elementary classes, leaving him a great deal of time to "wander" while waiting to be challenged by his teachers. His penchant for "wandering" providing him the opportunity to see more of what the world had to offer. With high expectations of his parents and, more importantly, of himself, he navigated a world that was sometimes not a welcoming place for a young, driven black child. This did not deter him in the least.

I met Hank when he and I both worked at The Bowen Elementary School in Newton, Ma. I was a kindergarten teacher and he was the Physical Education instructor. At time, I had no idea how deep and meaningful a relationship we would develop over the years. Reading this book allowed me insight into a life that been in the process of "becoming" long before I met him.

Hank provides a detailed, almost day by day, moment by moment, experience by experience look into how and why he became the man he is today. I began to see that his attention to the most minute details that he provided served a purpose. We all have experienced victories and defeats, pain and sorrow, living up to expectations, feeling we've let others down. It's what you do with those experiences that determine how you live. Hank has taken many risks. He has chosen not to shy away from the controversial, whether it be in his professional life, or his personal relationships. His eye has always remained on the good that would come, not on the disappointment that can come to those who strive to find out how good they can be." FOHGYCB"

I found that Hank has always opted to choose the path that was most challenging. After a long career as an educator in the Newton Public Schools, his need to continue learning and growing was clear. A whole new career in adult education at Valencia College in Florida began to crystallize what had always been at the heart of his passion.

He teaches and champions issues related to DEI, Racism and Academic Achievement, Anti-Racist Training Sessions, as well as his work in the Peace and Justice Institute. This was where all of his early "wandering" in elementary school, the "twelve years in the making" that his father always eluded to, his attention to what might have seemed minuscule and unimportant to some, all of that has led to Hank being the person that he is today. Even now, as our times present obstacles to the very essence of what Hank has embraced his entire life, a digression into old tropes around race, equality and justice, he continues to do what he is known to encourage others to do, "stay up".

This is a book about determination, dedication to ones convictions, and striving to be better in the face of a sometimes hard and difficult world. I think we all find a little bit of ourselves in this book, as we sometimes win and sometimes lose. The important thing is in the trying. As Hank often says, "live the life you love and love the life you live".

I will close by saying that when I was in 5th grade, I too wanted to be a crossing guard because they got hot chocolate in the winter. I got the gig, the hot chocolate was good, but it wasn't all that. I think Hank got a lot more than hot chocolate.

Peace,
Kemp Harris

TABLE OF CONTENTS

YESTERDAYS

TWELVE YEARS OF TRYING

*I*t was the early 1960s, and the weather was just right for Halloween night. The sun had almost disappeared over the trees at the end of 139th Street and it was time for ghosts and goblins to appear.

"Mom, I got my pants rolled up, this shirt of Dad's that's WAY too big for me and the neckerchief on just right. But I need some help with putting on this make-up for the mustache to complete my pirate outfit… C'mon, mom, the kids are waiting at the door!"

"And they'll just have to wait a few minutes if you want me to do this right! Did you give them their treat from the bowl?"

"Not yet."

"Stand still and don't move while I finish." She paused for a moment. "Ahhh, there you go. You are the scariest pirate I've seen and the best dressed, too."

"Hank, c'mon! What's taking so long?" Craig bellowed from the steps of our front porch in his pirate outfit. "We got some treats to pick up."

"Yeah, Hank, let's go!" Charles, wearing a Frankenstein mask, Gary dressed as Buckwheat from the kids show I grew up watching The Little Rascals and Clyde, decked out like the very tall butler, Lurchfrom ghoulish TV show the Addams Family, all chimed in.

I opened the door and held out the bowl for my buds to grab a handful. My parents were always generous with giving out candy on Halloween. A large plastic bowl was filled with almond joy, assorted candy bars, sweet-n-sours, mini bags of Swedish fish, tootsie rolls, lollipops and so much more.

After placing the bowl back on the table next to the door, I grabbed my UNICEF box to collect money for children in need throughout the world. Since 1946, the United Nations Children's Emergency Fund (UNICEF) has worked tirelessly to meet the emergency needs of children in Europe and China after World War II. Collecting donations for them at Halloween was a way for us to give back.

With the box in hand, I picked up the pillowcase that Mom had left on a chair by the door to hold whatever treats I was given. Out the door I went and jumped from the top of the stoop onto the pavement. We all headed up one side of 139th Street. When we got to the end of the cul-de-sac, we crossed over and headed down the other side. We took turns ringing each home's doorbell and would all shout out "trick or treat for UNICEF" as the front door of a house opened to a smiling adult where another big bowl of candy awaited.

There were kids everywhere, dashing back and forth across the street from one house to another.

"Mrs. Holland has got the Oh Henry's," Carol dressed as the Wicked Witch from The Wizard of Oz, announced from across the street.

"The McRae's let me take two handfuls," Freddie, Craig's younger brother, wearing sailor suit, joyously proclaimed.

"Let's go to my house." Jean, in her Sleeping Beauty outfit beckoned. "My mom has got some really cool lollipops!"

When I got to Craig's house, his mom, Mrs. Milan, gave me a nickel for the unfortunate kids to put into my collection box. By night's end, I'd have over a dollar in pennies, nickels, dimes and a few quarters.

The sun had set by now, the streetlights were all aglow and the flashlights we each held helped to light the path as we neared the alley just before 109th Avenue. We saw, what we thought, were two little girls we didn't recognize from another neighborhood walking toward us. And we thought we could scare them and take some of their candy.

"Hey, what you got in that bag?" Michael fronted.

"Yeah, let's see what you got," Clyde said in a made-up voice that was deeper than his natural way of speaking as he tried to sound older.

We began to surround the two, when one of the girls stepped forward and fronted back. "You don't want any of this candy. I think you should give us yours!"

Suddenly, three other older kids appeared from the dimly lit alleyway and doubled down. "Yeah, you better give us your candy or this knuckle sandwich will have your name on it."

Faster than a speeding bullet, more powerful than a locomotive, and able to leap tall buildings in a single bound, we took off running in the opposite direction post haste, clinging to our collection of candy, my UNICEF box of coins jingling with each stride.

What a yesterday that was.

I grew up in New York City, Jamaica, Queens, about a mile and a half from Kennedy Airport on the Van Wyck Expressway, between Liberty Avenue and Linden Boulevard. It was a different time, back in the late 50s and throughout the 60s, when I lived on the close-knit cul-de-sac of 139th Street. It was a time when everyone on the block looked out for the children of others.

My first memory of who I was came in the springtime of 1956 or 57. I was four, maybe five years old. My dad, a taxi driver, was taking me with him on the day shift, one Saturday morning. When we arrived at the taxi garage, he introduced me to a coworker.

"Aw, c'mon, Stafford. He looks too good to be your son," I remember the co-worker responded.

"Yeah, maybe so," my dad replied. "But he's the product of *twelve years of trying*," my dad proudly announced.

It wasn't until some years later that I understood what *twelve years of trying* really meant. Beginning with my elementary grade school years, the tag of *twelve years of trying* always came right after my name… like when I started kindergarten.

"Hello, Mrs. Wood. This is our son Henry. He's the product of twelve years of trying." But it was the next statement that has stayed with me to this day.

"If he gives you any trouble," with a wag of his index finger, "just let us know."

LET'S START FROM THE VERY BEGINNING: P.S. 160 QUEENS

We'd line up in the school yard at our stenciled-in-white painted-on asphalt room number. In each classroom, there were five rows of six bolted-to-the-floor desks, four huge windows with dozens of panes of glass, and a big sliding door closet on the opposite side of the room where we'd hang our coats. The entire school shared one playground ball–or so it seemed to me at the time for any recess outside. Cathy, a girl in my class through the third grade, lived catty-corner from the school. She was late almost every day.

The first school I attended was P.S. 160, on Inwood Street, for grades K-3. Today, the name of my former school, P.S. 160, has been changed to the Walter Francis Bishop Magnet School of the Arts. It was about a mile walk from home. I remember the names of my elementary school teachers: Mrs. Wood (Kindergarten), Mrs. Grosotti (first grade), Mrs. Kelly (second grade), and Mrs. Kutensky (third grade).

In addition to letting my teachers know of their efforts to bring me into this world, my parents, in the next sentence, also let them know to use "any means necessary… let us know if he misbehaves," to keep me in line with theirs and the school's expectations. I interpreted this to mean that someone would knock me into the middle of next week if I didn't properly comply. But, both of my parents said this in a different way. My dad would often say, "Make yourself desirable so that people will want to have you around." Everything I tell you is for your own good." While my mom would always encourage me to "Be the best version of yourself in all you do." I continue to model these messages to my children, grandchildren, great-grandchildren, along with the students and adults that I interact with to this day.

Cookies and warm milk at mid-morning snack time are good for you. And along with the classroom sandbox were a couple of the easygoing memories of my first year in school; be it only half a day.

These times saw students being dismissed at noon to go home for lunch. So, beginning in 1st grade, Dad, who worked nights driving a taxi back then, would greet me in our 1955 gray Chevy four door in front of the school at noontime. And then off to lunch at home, which often turned out to be a study session with Dad. There were always spelling words and math problems, and one lunchtime while I was in the 2nd grade, I had to gather materials for a science experiment to be done at school. Dad had to put a pinhole in both ends of an egg, and then he blew out the insides. *Good grief!* I don't recall what the experiment was back at school, but I did manage to get the eggshell back intact for the afternoon's class that started around 1 PM. All the while, I was trying to enjoy my bowl of Campbell's pepper pot soup, and a glass of chocolate milk. My first, favorite lunch.

I was fast in completing my work at school; more often than not, it was correct. My problems grew from this capacity to finish quickly and accurately because I didn't know what to do with my time once done. I don't think Mrs. Grosotti was ready for me to be done so quickly either. Anyway, I'd walk around the room, look out one of the four big windows, watch the sweep hand go around the clock, distract classmates, break my pencil point so that I would have to resharpen it, or get permission to go to the bathroom, and take myself on a tour of the building… you know, the usual things fast working students tend to do.

In September 1959, I entered the second grade, Mrs. Kelly, Room 202. The movie *SLEEPING BEAUTY* was a box office success and I was hoping to see it. One Saturday morning, my mom and I ventured into midtown Manhattan on the E-train only to find that the movie was sold out for that day. Mom, being the forward thinker she was, inquired about the next morning which was Sunday. She secured two tickets, though, for a late morning viewing on the next day, and this time we walked right in.

We lived about a mile from PS 160, and I would walk there with my friend Ronald, an older neighborhood friend and Crossing Guard Captain at P.S. 160. One morning, during 2nd grade on our way to school, a single-family house was on fire. We stopped to look from a safe distance away for a moment, but soon we were on our way, so as not to be late. Coincidentally, my mother passed by the same situation while riding on the Q40 of the Green Bus Line on her way to work. When she arrived at her job that day, she called school to be sure that I had arrived on time. This was before the time of cell phones, so she had to wait until she got off the bus to use a public telephone. Good thing she always carried a dime for such occasions; lessons learned to always be prepared.

Sometimes, Ronald's teacher, Mr. Hollander, would drive by on his way to school. Ronald belonged to a specially selected group of boys who made sure we crossed the street safely in front of the school. And sometimes, Ronald's teacher would offer him a ride for the final two or three blocks, but not me. This always seemed odd to me at the time. But on reflection years later, this was during the time immediately after the 1954 Brown v. Board of Education Supreme Court Decision, which ruled that the state laws establishing segregation in public schools were unconstitutional. The NYC Public Schools were in the process of upholding the decision. However, at P.S 160, our entire class was composed of young Black minds, waiting to be developed. I'd later find out that desegregating its schools was a difficult undertaking for the NYC Public Schools. Ironically, today, some states and school districts continue to try and skirt this decision in more subtle ways such as with Charter Schools and school vouchers. Maybe Mr. Hollander believed it was okay to have one Black student ride in his car, but not two.

Mrs. Kelly, who was my first Black teacher and always dressed for success, seemed to think that there were only two children in the entire class. "That girl" or "That boy" (with an emphatic accent on the final "t") in a stern, booming voice was her way of getting everyone's attention in a hurry. Because she had such wonderful skills as a teacher, I did a lot less wandering in the second grade. And, as a Black woman, she looked like us. I recall that year when any one of her students was out ill for more than a day, we would all write a 'get-well' letter to our classmate. Mrs. Kelly would include one, too, then put it in the mail. And, so we wouldn't be too sick for too long, a good chunk of the day's schoolwork was in the mailer with the letters.

Mrs. Kelly brought her own camera to take a class picture of us when we planted a live tree on Arbor Day in April of that school year. Dancing around the Maypole tree on May Day was another part of the culture of P.S. 160.

One uncomfortable experience remains fresh in my mind from second grade. I found myself betwixt and between the proverbial rock and a hard place with my fellow classmates. Here's what happened.

One part of each school day was for reading instruction. As such, in our basal reader, we often read aloud in front of the entire class. This was bad enough for everybody. One day, as a classmate was reading, she got stuck on the pronunciation of a word. *Stir.* Mrs. Kelly went from child to child, down one row and up the next, to find someone who could correctly pronounce *stir.* Being asked to correctly spell a word at any time, was immediately followed by the student demonstrating how the word was used in the sentence. Maybe Mrs. Kelly knew that I knew what she was looking for. Maybe it was because my last name, Van Putten, put me near the back of the final row of desks. Whatever the reason, I was the last person she called on. I correctly pronounced the word and described its use in a sentence. Mrs. Kelly then proceeded to publicly lambaste my peers, my friends, kids I had to play with, about their lack of readiness to go on to the next chapter in the reader, and how I was the only one who "got it" and was ready to move on. Kids were then, are today, and will be tomorrow, kids. So, my classmates only stayed angry with me for, what seemed like, forever!

There was a local TV kids show on WNEW called Wonderama. Part of the programming included a spelling bee. And of course, my dad would test my spelling skills whenever we watched together.

"Say it," Dad would firmly request in his military voice.

I would.

"Spell it," he would urge me in the same tone.

I'd do likewise.

"Now use it in a sentence," was always the third step.

This was sometimes challenging, but doing so would have benefits that my young mind could not yet imagine.

"Everything I tell you is for your own good," he would often tell me.

Years later, I had the privilege to visit Mrs. Kelly while I was in college. She made a big deal of it for the current students who probably didn't know how blessed they were to have her as their teacher. Just as she looked like to us when I was in 2nd grade-a successful Black woman-she pointed to me to her students as someone who was on the pathway to success. A young Black man who looked like them. It felt amazing to be honored in this way, and to pay it forward to those young minds, as Mrs. Kelly had done for us.

I was assigned to Mrs. Kutensky, Room 313, for the third grade. Ronald and I started out walking to school most mornings and on those occasions when Mr. Hollander picked him up, I walked the rest of the way alone. Ronald wore his blue and silver shield on a white guard belt that went over one shoulder, around his waist and had a neat buckle in the front. I don't know how many guards there were at P.S. 160. What I did know was that I couldn't wait. I dreamed of being in the fifth grade to have a chance to be a patrolman, the entry level role for a Crossing Guard. This could lead to Sergeant or Lieutenant by the sixth grade! I figured hanging around with the Crossing Guard Captain would help me climb the ladder of success, even give me a leg up. By the end of that 3rd grade year, though, this dream came crashing down like the house of sticks in the Three Little Pigs.

Third grade was the first time that I remember that we had to practice fire drills. Everybody did, and still does as a routine part of school safety. Unfortunately, in our current world, the need to also practice 'shelter in place drills' and 'lockdown' is a part of this routine.

The air-raid siren, a leftover relic from World War 2, planted atop the school, would begin to blare its sound.

"Stay away from the windows! Out into the hallway!" was always the command from Mrs. Kutensky. Everyone would immediately stop their work, move into the hallway, line up along the wall, squat down, and cover our heads with our hands and arms (similar to the crash-landing position on an airplane, but without sitting down) until the siren stopped a minute or two later.

Comparatively speaking, Mrs. Kutensky was a lamb compared to Mrs. Kelly. She wore glasses and was always smiling as she circulated around the classroom. Maybe that's why I started wandering again. I knew the school's layout quite well by then. I was still in the last row, next to the last seat, with a good view out the window. Mrs. Kutensky, though, continued to challenge me with our schoolwork in similar ways that Mrs. Kelly had done the previous year. Being able to meet and exceed her expectations would turn out to be tied to my Crossing Guard dream dissolving.

After I had visited Mrs. Kelly that day years later as a college student, I made it a point to do likewise for Mrs. Kutensky before I left the building. It was a joy to see her response in seeing me coming back. Like Mrs. Kelly, she introduced me to her current students with the same enthusiasm that I had just been afforded a few rooms away.

It was late May or early June of 1961, and Flag Day was still a holiday on or around June 14th. The dream of the New York Mets joining the National League of Major League Baseball was gaining momentum. They would replace the departed Giants who had left the city in 1957 for San Francisco. My dad had taken me to their final game at the Polo Grounds in upper Manhattan, across the East/Harlem River from Yankee Stadium. The Pittsburgh Pirates won 9-1. It was during the game that I learned from my dad how to keep score at a baseball game. I kept up this practice of keeping score for years to come while attending games at Shea Stadium, Yankee Stadium or Fenway Park, or sitting in my living room watching games on our black and white television.

Keeping score at a baseball game brings the action to life in a sport where there is seemingly not much going on most of the time. Just like the Abbott and Costello routine of *WHO'S ON FIRST*, each player on the field is identified by a number, not the one on the back of their uniform but by the position on the field each is playing:

1. Pitcher
2. Catcher
3. First baseman

4. Second baseman
5. Third baseman
6. Shortstop
7. Left fielder
8. Center fielder
9. Right fielder

The scorecard, found inside and at the centerfold of the game's program (fifty cents), was a blank page that had room for the players name on the left, and then a grid of boxes about half-an-inch each, to record what the batter had done. Across the top were the innings numbered from 1 to 9.

For example, a ground ball out to the shortstop who threw to the first baseman was recorded as "6-3" inside the box next to the player's name in the inning they were batting. A flyball caught for an out to the center fielder was "8." A swinging strikeout shown as "K," and a strikeout looking, a *backwards K*. A walk, or base on balls, was "BB." A batter who reached base via a hit (single, double, or triple) would read "-7 or =9" and I used "HR" for home run. Others I knew would use "HOP" (hit out of park) for a homerun. If there were a DP (double play out) I'd have to write small to get in, for example, the "6-4-3."

There were several other nuances in keeping score that my dad showed me. When a pitching change happened, I'd draw a dark line along two sides of the box of the last batter the pitcher had faced. When a pinch-hitter took the place of another, I'd carefully put the player's number, the one on his back, next to the box.

Something was always going on, even when it appeared there was a lull in the action. When a fast-running batter reached first base, the second baseman and shortstop would silently and quickly communicate before each pitch which of the two would cover the base if the runner tried to steal. A quick glance at each other, using their glove to cover their face to everyone by showing an open mouth meant "you" cover, lips pursed together meant "me," *I'll cover*. It happened with such nonchalance that if you blinked, you'd miss how they were communicating.

I stood for the playing of the National Anthem in my living room as a young child, and had a notebook full of games I had kept score of. In later years, when I'd go to a game with colleagues, knowing that I kept score, they'd often ask me how the batter had done earlier in the game. Here's what it looks like on the scorecard.

Unlike The Amazins (a nickname tagged to the New York Mets by Manager Casey Stengel) though, my dream of becoming a Crossing Guard was dealt a fatal blow that spring. It seemed that four other "ready" classmates and myself were about to be rewarded for our capacity to learn by being transferred to the Intellectually Gifted Children (I.G.C.) program, out of district, at P.S. 123. All the hard work I had put in toward becoming a Crossing Guard was erased by my capacity to learn in school, as demonstrated by some kind of standardized test. It seemed so unfair. We cried with our classmates for what seemed like all the way to the end of the school year. How could they take away my big opportunity to be a Crossing Guard, *just* to be in an Intellectually Gifted Children's class?

I.G.C. CLASS

With the beginning of fourth grade, there were some important changes that took place.

First, to get to P.S 123 where my I.G.C. class was, I had to take the bus to school. Not the traditional yellow school bus, but public transportation on the Q-40 of the Green Bus Lines. Initially, my parents thought they would need to give me thirty cents a day for my round-trip bus ride. But for those of us riding on the Green Bus Line, we'd get a new pass every month in a different color. All I had to do was show it to the driver and find a seat. Crossing Guard Captain couldn't touch this new privilege. I'd leave with my mom each morning since we would be taking the same Q-40 bus, albeit going in opposite directions on the route.

Second, I was nine years old and my parents wanted me to join the boys' choir at Grace Episcopal Church, where we worshiped on Sundays. And it was Ronald, now former Captain of the Crossing Guards, who made sure I got there and back home safely. Both my parents could more than carry a tune. I'd often hear them singing along to a melody on the radio, or on our black and white television to *Sing Along With Mitch* (Miller) or *The Lawrence Welk Show*, or *The Ed Sullivan Show*. Also, a lot of Nat King Cole and Frank Sinatra. Mom was a beautiful soprano and dad in the deepest baritone. One Sunday afternoon, they took me to a recital of a friend of theirs who had a booming baritone voice. I'm surprised I remember much about the singer because I was enthusiastically and emphatically mouthing their words, and their body language, right from my aisle seat looking directly at them. Suddenly, I felt the fingers of my mom pinching my left ear to get me to stop what I was doing.

Joining the Grace Church Choir would turn out to be the start of one of the wonderful experiences in my life. It would last until I graduated high school, eight years later. I'm going to tell you more about my time in the choir in a bit.

Being in the fourth grade I.G.C. class at P.S.123 brought additional changes to my daily routine. One was okay, the other was a burden. Regarding the former, I no longer went home for lunch. It was nice having a thermos, filled with chocolate milk or lemonade or pepper pot soup, a peanut butter and jelly sandwich and a piece of fruit. No more home lunchtime with Dad. I think I went through a good 4 or 5 of those thermoses early that school year. The inside of the thermos was made of glass. Me being me, I'd invariably drop my lunch box or toss it to the side of the playground and wind up with a thermos full of my favorite soup mixed with pieces of glass. Mom wasn't pleased with me each each time it happened. After the third time, she sternly gave me a choice. If I wanted to enjoy my favorite soup or beverage with my lunch each day, I'd have to do a better job of transporting and taking care of the thermos at school. A tall task and another lesson learned-take care of your belongings

Another change in my daily routine was having to wear a tie every day *and* my dad insisted that I learn to tie it myself. Actually, I had been wearing a tie since Kindergarten, the kind that had a hook and mom just latched it over my collar where my button, buttoned at my throat. Now, in 4th grade, I had to learn to tie my own tie.

Years later, when I became an administrator, I had to talk my son and namesake, Hank III, through tying his tie at school over the telephone. As a member of his high school basketball team, players were required to wear a shirt and tie to school on the day of a game, be it home or away. If the coach saw them in school without one, sitting on the bench and not playing was a distinct possibility. He was at school, between classes, and in a bit of a panic when he called me around 9 AM at work. Hank had his tie with him, but he'd forgotten how to tie his tie properly and needed my help. Less than five minutes later, over the phone, I taught him as my dad had taught me.

Hank loved basketball and at age eleven, he had earned a spot on a travel team. During one game, he went up high to block an opponent's shot and got undercut by the shooter, landing on his wrist. OUCH! An ice pace was applied and we headed to the emergency room about fifteen minutes away. He was immediately seen and an X-ray taken that revealed a dislocation. The attending doctor told me he'd have to give Hank some medicine (demerol) so that the dislocation could be reduced back into place. He sat on the examining table, got the medicine in his arm, and we waited for its effect to set in.

Less than five minutes later, Hank looked over to me with a wry smile that I had never seen before, and uttered in a voice I had not heard before, "That's some good medicine." After reducing the joint and applying a cast, getting the doctor to sign it, we headed home.

That was quite the yesterday.

At P.S. 123, the color of your tie seemed to me to be an indication of the grade you were in, like an identification badge. I forget what the fourth grade color was, but I do remember that fifth grade was red, and sixth grade was blue.

Being an intellectually gifted child didn't seem like that big of a deal. Classroom desks were aligned in rows and my seat was still at the back of the last row. We still hung our coats in the big closet with the sliding door and there were four big windows. Our room number was stenciled-in paint on the playground.

In I.G.C. class (Mrs. Samuels for fourth, Miss Shepherd for fifth and Mrs. Newman for sixth grade) we had a Spanish lesson with Mrs. Musille as part of our weekly schoolwork. How many times a week, and for how long each class, I don't recall. But I can tell you that after three years with Mrs. Musille, I could count to one hundred, use general greetings, and say my name. As I've gone through the yesterdays of my life cycle, I pause every now and then to reflect on any regrets that I had about a particular moment in the past. I wonder if given the opportunity, how I would do things differently. Not learning another world language to fluency in my public-school years, is one of my biggest regrets.

Fourth grade was the first year that a professional photographer came to school to take pictures. In our fourth grade photo, Mrs. Samuels, our teacher, stood nervously with us at one end of the back row.

This was the first time that I felt my teacher didn't know how to teach us. By us, I mean black students. Mrs. Samuels tried to be too authoritarian in interactions with us. There was an absence of genuine caring, even the kind of tough love I had experienced with Mrs. Kelly. She retired at the end of that school year. Many of my classmates teased me by saying that I was the cause of her leaving because I wandered around the school and classroom so much. Just like in 1st grade, when my work was done and there was no plan, I filled the time as I saw fit, just as I had done at P.S. 160. One afternoon, I spent almost the entire time before dismissal in the guidance counselor's office because someone was announcing who my girlfriend was in the classroom. Mrs. Samuels didn't know what to do with me other than ask me to leave. I probably gave back a few "No she's not," to the peers teasing me, but I left and was out of the classroom for the afternoon.

Years later, when I was teaching middle school physical education, there were occasions when I'd have to consider sending a student out of the classroom. But I thought harder on how I would bring them back to the learning environment. That kind of reflection allowed me to expand my repertoire of "attention and momentum" strategies (*THE SKILLFUL TEACHER*, Saphier, Gower) and keep the student in the classroom. One year teaching middle school PE, I did send a student out of class and to the office. Sue, an administrator colleague came back a few minutes later with the student and commented to them, "You must have really crossed the line because Mr. Van Putten never sends students to see me."

I began playing a musical instrument, the trumpet, in the school band in fourth grade. I remember Shaun on the clarinet. Jenny with the flute. Louis needed another reed for his saxophone. Dante on the trombone. And Mr. Fallon the band teacher. A stout, bald-headed white man who could play a mean trumpet! That's why I initially chose the trumpet. But I soon got tired of the case banging my leg while walking to and from the bus stop. Carrying this extra weight with my lunchbox, notebook and other school equipment was not going to work!

By the middle of the year, I switched to something that matched my need for expression. The kind of expression that wandering the hallways often afforded me. Playing the drums only required me to carry a pair of drumsticks. *Much better.* Mr. Fallon took the best 5 or 6 players and formed a jazz/dance band, and they needed a drummer which I was glad to step up to do.

We had eraser vacuums at P.S. 123. During these days a blackboard was in each classroom for the teacher to write on using chalk. No tablets or smart boards back then. Over the course of the day, whenever our teacher erased the blackboard, a good bit of chalk from the blackboard would accumulate in each of the two, felt erasers. These had to be cleaned at the end of the school day.

An eraser vacuum was a pipe, topped by a soap dish like platter with an on/off handle like the water shut off for the kitchen sink at home. They were located at the end of the corridor on the school's top floor. Around 2:50 PM every day, the eraser monitors in several classrooms would gather at this area together to clean erasers with the efficiency of a Hoover vacuum, including sound. Then, one day in fourth grade when it was my responsibility to clean our classroom erasers, the system didn't work. I don't remember whose idea it was, but I happily followed along as we all trekked down to the first-floor exit, went outside, and played eraser dust tag clapping two erasers together. They got just as clean as they would have using a vacuum. Mrs. Samuels and everyone else wanted to know how we had managed to get chalk dust all over ourselves. We looked so white when we returned for dismissal.

Mom bought me a brand-new red tie to begin fifth grade I.G.C. year with Miss Shepard. She was a tall bespeckled, yet statuesque black woman with an engaging smile, who commanded your attention and respect. Dad had been working with me throughout the previous year on learning how to make a Windsor knot. Having to wear a tie five days a week and on Sunday for church gave me a chance to practice a lot. To be honest, I had no choice in the matter.

The resemblance in teaching styles, and appearance (both were black women) between Miss Shepard and Mrs. Kelly, kept my attention. There was no more wandering. Gloria Ladson-Billings has researched and written about the importance of making connections with students in an authentic way. The strategies and accompanying stories in her book, *THE DREAMKEEPERS*, demonstrates what this authenticity looks like. Author, Chris Emdin, refers to this authenticity as employing a reality pedagogy to the teaching practice. There was a real "family" approach to learning in 5 I.G.C. Miss Shepard was a creative educator who took risks that resulted in providing a challenging and realistic classroom environment. In more than one "unit" of study we worked with others as part of a team. This kind of *collaborative* education, where decision-making and partnership work in tandem, provided a co-operative learning environment where students were responsible to each other for the success of everyone.

Unfortunately for me, my parents had proudly told Miss Shepard that I sang in our church's boys' choir. I promise, I'm going to tell you more about my choir experience in a little bit. For now, it's important for you to know that at the end of my first year in the choir, Mr. Amend, the choirmaster, recognized me as the outstanding new soprano. I wore a special medallion at every service on a red ribbon around my neck. It was quite the honor to wear one and my mom, who worked as a jeweler, had my name engraved on the back of the medallion, HENRY STAFFORD VAN PUTTEN JR

Miss Shepard, whom to the best of my knowledge had never heard me sing a note, proceeded to volunteer me to Mrs. Nadelman, the principal, to sing the national anthem over the schools' public address system at school. It wasn't *every day,* but as I write this thought out to you, I can still see the PA microphone in front of me, and the bar on its bottom for me to press and hold down while singing. On these occasions, I sang from memory what I thought was the first and second verses of the anthem. It wouldn't be until years later that I found out that what I thought was verse two, was really verse four.

What? Why wasn't I told about this back then? I asked myself. Whenever the anthem was played, and I'd stand before a baseball game, only the first verse was sung. *And what, then, did the second and third verses say and why they were skipped over?*

I've given a talk to multi-aged groups entitled "Kaepernick and the National Anthem" during Justice Week at Valencia College and at the Black Brown and College Bound Conference. A part of the talk has the attendees examine the words of the second and third verses of the anthem while having an authentic conversation in small groups about their perspective on the meaning of the words. The evidence of systemic oppression in the third verse is always an "AHA" moment for folks. Many do not know how many verses of the anthem there are, and are equally surprised when learning of the second and third verses. Here are these two rarely sung or heard verses:

Verse <u>II</u>

On the shore, dimly seen through the mists of the deep,
Where the foe's haughty host in dread silence reposes,
What is that which the breeze, o'er the towering steep,
As it fitfully blows, half conceals, half discloses?
Now it catches the gleam of the morning's first beam,
In full glory reflected now shines on the stream:
'Tis the star-spangled banner! O long may it wave
O'er the land of the free and the home of the brave.

Verse <u>III</u>

And where is that band who so vauntingly swore,
That the havoc of war and the battle's confusion,
A home and a country should leave us no more?
Their blood has wiped out their foul footstep's pollution.
No refuge could save the hireling and slave,
From the terror of flight, or the gloom of the grave:
And the star-spangled banner in triumph doth wave,
O'er the land of the free and the home of the brave.

Most of the fifth and sixth grade I.G.C (with Mrs. Newman for sixth grade) went by fast. A sure sign that I was enjoying the time. Some school memories over those two years have stayed with me. Like our cultural exchange experience with students at a public school in Chinatown. Their class spent a day with us in Queens, and we were invited to do likewise in Manhattan. We'd stay in touch with a 'pen-pal' over the rest of the school year.

Our class went on several other field trips over those two school years. One was to a local dining spot in Jamaica, Queens for lunch. We had a lesson on using a menu beforehand, so we'd know what and how to order upon arriving. A life skill. We went on field trips that saw us go to the Statue of Liberty, the American Museum of Natural History, The Hayden Planetarium, to the top of the Empire State Building, and to the Metropolitan Museum of Art on the occasion of the Mona Lisa being on display. I really enjoyed these opportunities to travel around the city (wander) to see new places and have new learning experiences in many different hospitable communities

As the end of 5th grade approached, it was made known that classroom space, because of larger enrollment at P.S. 123, was an issue. And when it was announced that 6 I.G.C. would be housed in one of the brand-new portable classrooms… well, such a privilege would be like becoming Captain of the Crossing Guards all over again! In the end, though, we would wind up in Room 319. Another disappointment.

One day during the fall of sixth grade, there was a lot of uneasy commotion amongst the adults in the building. The non-verbal message that we were picking up was that someone we knew, an adult, had been involved in an accident that resulted in serious injury. I saw women in the office and a parent there too, in tears. I wondered what could have happened to bring on such emotion. Since it was lunchtime, there was a certain freedom that sixth graders had about the building. I hastily made my rounds.The principal and assistant principal were in their respective offices, the guidance counselor was accounted for, and I had seen Mrs. Newman, our classroom teacher, go into the teachers' room for lunch. What was going on? We all wanted to know, on that day, November 22, 1963.

Before dismissal that afternoon, we were informed over the school's PA system that the President had been seriously hurt. However, as parents were gathering outside for dismissal, the news began to spread quickly that John F. Kennedy had been assassinated. When I got home and told my grandmother of the news, she initially didn't believe me. When she turned on the television, her worst fears were confirmed.

I remember learning how to ride a bike, and taking some adventurous rides when I was in elementary school. Having a bike at age seven brought a sense of freedom. My first bike was a foot brake model that required reverse pressure on the pedals to stop the bike. I enjoyed the freedom that my bike presented. I kept it in our garage at the far end of the driveway. Then, each time I went for a ride, I'd begin by riding down our driveway, slowly tap backwards on the pedals as I got to the closed gate without stopping, and carefully bump into the closed gate without dismounting. Then in a perfectly timed motion, I would fling the gate back so it would close without stopping or getting off of my bike. Up and down our cul-de-sac, I'd go as fast as possible.

However, my biggest short fall in taking care of my bike was that I had a penchant for riding through potholes in the road which resulted in the front fork of my bike to bend. My dad would try to straighten the fork out a few times, and he'd warn me that if I wasn't more careful, I'd wind up going head-over the handlebar. Of course I didn't listen, and after flying over the handlebar, I wound up with a nicely scraped up nose for not heeding his wisdom.

On my ninth birthday I was given a Schwinn, a three-speed bike with hand brakes. As an added bonus, it turned out to be that after owning it for a year, on my tenth birthday my dad took it to the bike shop to add a derailleur to both the front and back sprockets of my bike. I now had a nine-speed bike, and these modifications gave me a good deal of added speed.

One place where my friends and I would ride to was about two miles from home on a busy, major street called Hillside Avenue. Many of the side streets that fed into this thoroughfare were hilly and provided the need-for-speed and thrills we sought, as we careened toward a busy intersection. You really had to have good brakes as one's life was literally on the line approaching Hillside Avenue and trying to make it to the traffic light before it turned red in our direction.

There were three parks and playgrounds within two miles of our street that we would frequent, especially on weekends. Sunnyside Park had three basketball hoops along a long fence abutting the service road of the Van Wyck, a blacktop with baseball markings, some seesaws, swings, and monkey bars.

I first visited Sunnyside at age three, as a toddler. The issue, though, was that I did it alone and without my parents knowing. You can imagine their worry and grief when they discovered I was not in the back yard, nor in front of the house or anywhere in the neighborhood. You see, I had gotten on my tricycle, and using the sidewalks, started to wander until I wound up at Sunnyside Playground where my parents finally and fortunately caught up to me.

Ajax Park was a straight line walk or ride down 139th Street from our home. At Ajax, there was a playground *way* across two baseball fields that I don't ever recall using. The combined area of the two fields is where we played football on the manicured outfield grass of the two baseball diamonds. It was always tackle football, using our own shoulder pads, a helmet, and whatever we could find lying around to mark where the end zone was. This was great and a lot more realistic than the two-hand-touch we'd play on the street of 107th Rd, which ran perpendicular to 139th Street.

My dad liked to make kites and would take me to Ajax to fly them. One weekend afternoon, the new one he had just finished was grabbed by a big gust of wind and landed in the telephone wires next to the park. That kite stayed there for weeks until a linesman or telephone worker finally took it down.

Then there was Lincoln Park. Still equidistant from home as the others, but we had to cross over the Van Wyck on the sidewalk on the way. This one was probably my favorite. It had swings, see-saw, monkey bars, a grass field where we'd play baseball and football, and handball courts. The courts were two tall cement slabs (making four courts in total), about 12-15 feet high and a foot thick. Picture the white lines for singles play on a tennis court. Similar lines marked the boundaries of the handball court. The serve or 'short' line' was where you stood to serve and to put the ball in play. The ball had to clear this line, a good 15-20 feet from the cement wall, if the serve was legal and within the rules. We used a round, pink ball for play. There was a status among my peers, and those friends (all black children) whom we'd meet there about one's handball skills. My hand-eye coordination was pretty good, as evidenced by staying on the court for multiple matches (games were to 21 points, and you have to win by two) before tiring. I was quite adept at being able to strike the ball with my open hand as close as possible to the bottom of the slab, making a return almost impossible for my opponent.

One afternoon, my friends and I traversed two miles through the streets of Jamaica, passing Linden and Rockaway Boulevards, crossing over the Belt Parkway, then passing the garage for the Green Bus Line, down a sparsely populated street. We wound up at a fence that marked the end of one of the runways at Kennedy Airport. Skillfully, we found a way through the fence, bikes in tow, and were suddenly on the end of the asphalt, where the white lines mark the beginning of the runway. As a jet approached for landing, we waved to the pilots as they passed overhead just before landing. After about three or four 727s and 707s flew less than 100 feet overhead, we retraced our steps. Making a quick exit and headed back to 139th Street before any pilot had a chance to let anyone know we were there.

When I was ten, my parents took me on a trip with them to St. Kitts in the Caribbean Dutch West Indies, the island where my dad had grown up. We also visited nearby Nevis, and the birthplace of Alexander Hamilton. It was my first time flying in one of those big jets that we'd seen that day. I even got to sit in the cockpit of one of those jets during our flight back home. I remember the stewardess coming through the cabin to take children, one or two at a time, to the front of the plane. There, she introduced me to the co-pilot who got up and asked me to take his seat at the controls. *Whoa!!* After sitting down amongst a sea of instruments, screens, and dials, he asked me if I'd like to put the jet on course for the airport. *Double whoa!* He then carefully guided my hand to a knob, and instructed me to "slowly, turn it to the right at 3:00." I did, ever so slowly, and the big jet began to bank in one direction. Still holding my hand, where my thumb and index finger were holding the knob, together we ever so slowly reversed the direction of the bank with a slow turn back to 12:00. *Triple whoa!* When I returned to my seat, my parents were enjoying a glass of wine and a snack. My excitement must have been beaming throughout the cabin when my mom asked me if I'd enjoyed my little excursion.

"Did you feel the plane when it tipped like this and back like this?" My eyes were lit up as I moved my arms to mimic a plane banking in one direction, then another. Before either could respond, I all but shouted out, "That was me turning the plane!"

They didn't believe me and thought I was making something up. Fortunately, the stewardess was nearby to overhear our conversation (probably through my exuberance) and told my parents that it had indeed happened. My mom seemed to acquiesce, but my dad remained steadfast as he took another sip of wine from his glass.

"Can I taste that?" I asked him.

"Sure," my dad replied with a wry smile.

"Stafford, no." My mom jumped in.

"It won't hurt him," my dad retorted. "I still don't think he turned the plane."

I took a sip from his glass. Maybe that's why I don't like dry wine today, as it tasted like sand.

That was quite a yesterday.

ALMOST ANGELS

*F*ather Crocker, a short, stocky gentleman who was the parish assistant to Father Lewis, was almost finished with his sermon. I knew this because from my seat in the choir stall, his notes for the sermon were in clear view to me.

The boys in the choir liked Father Crocker's sermons. He could really hold our attention with his wit, humor, and practical application of his words to our lives. He'd often remind the congregation of the words from the 23rd Psalm and the importance of placing our trust in God who would always be there for us. That, though, wasn't the reason we liked his sermons so much. They were relatively short, two or three typed, double-spaced pages. And my seat in the choir stall almost allowed me to read the words on the lectern. His sermons were brief and right to the point, which meant that the service was just about over.

On the other hand, Father Lewis, the parish rector, would talk… and talk… and talk. Page after page of typed single-spaced text. How could he write and read all of that? Wonder if he practiced like we had to do in the choir? I remember a story he once told around Christmas about World War II and him being part of the liberation of the real Stalag 13. The 'stalags' were German, prisoner of war camps during World War II. If you've ever watched the television show *HOGAN'S HEROES*, that will ring a bell for you.

Some of the gentlemen in the tenor and bass section would take 'forty-winks' whenever Father Lewis was giving a sermon. Even Mr. Amend, our choirmaster, would turn his light off and leave his seat at the organ keyboard for a stretch and more comfortable seat. Mr. Amend would always seem to reappear about the time we noticed the space on the last page of the sermon. The nudges would begin from person to person to 'wake up' as it was almost time for Father Lewis to give the blessing before we sang the recessional hymn. Then it was downstairs into the choir room to hang our vestments in our lockers, run back upstairs to the Sunday's sunshine to meet our parents in front of Grace Church, and then head home for the rest of Sunday afternoon with family, playtime, and finishing any leftover homework.

We were almost angels.

Ronald and I boarded the Q9 bus at the corner of Lincoln Street and 109th Avenue for the fifteen-minute or so ride to Jamaica Avenue and Parsons Boulevard where Grace Church is located. Being in the choir at Grace Church was a big deal in our community, which spread from South Jamaica where I lived, to Hollis, St. Albans, Springfield Gardens, Rosedale, Cambria Heights, Flushing and beyond.

I must humbly say with a sprinkle of bias, we were good! Our parents told us at every opportunity. So too, did Mr. Amend, Father Lewis, Father Crocker. And the Diocesan Bishop. We were often invited to give afternoon concerts at other parishes throughout Long Island and the New York City area.

Our choir was an official member of the Royal Church School of Music in London, England. Although we never traveled across the pond, we sang with other member choirs at an annual event held at the Cathedral of Saint John the Divine, in Manhattan.

Being in "the choir at Grace" made a statement for each of us. Our membership in the choir wasn't so much about a commitment to a religion, but rather about what children, especially young black boys, will do to be accepted in a group.

We spent part of four days each week at church: rehearsals after school on Tuesdays, Wednesdays, and Friday evenings, plus regular service on Sunday. Grace Church in Jamaica; founded in 1702, it is the oldest Episcopal church in Queens and the Diocese of Long Island. It did not have a religious school to draw from for choir membership. It was the adults in the community that directed us to form this affinity group of young singers. There were between fifteen and twenty of us who were sopranos, ages nine to fourteen, in the boy's choir. On Friday evenings, Mr. Lee would be waiting outside the church at 8 PM and gave his son Beef, Ronald and me a ride home. We called him Beef because he was so skinny, he needed to put-on-some-Beef.

I remember one Tuesday evening rehearsal in 1965. We were singing our little hearts out, bouncing each note off the roof of our mouths as we had been trained. I could actually feel the vibration, which almost tickled. The sound that reverberated off the choir room walls in the church basement where we practiced would often bring a smile to Mr. Amend's face as we sang. Just before 5:30 PM, as we were finishing up rehearsing Sunday's anthem, the lights went out. Startled, we paused as Mr. Amend found a nearby flashlight and went into the boiler room to find the fuse box. When he returned, we were still sitting there in the dark, music sheets in our laps. Not finding a solution to the darkness, he ended rehearsal. We all climbed the dark stairway and ventured out into the darkness and confusion happening on Jamaica Avenue at the height of rush hour. Bus and car headlights provided a bit of needed safety to see. The Q6, Q9 and the City bus Lines were still running, and police officers were doing their best to control the intersections, now without working traffic lights. Despite this chaos and confusion, I made it home safely as the blackout extended well into the night past my bedtime. The Northeast blackout of 1965 disrupted the supply of electricity from Ontario, Canada, throughout much of New England and into Pennsylvania, Maryland and Delaware.

Mr. Amend knew how to keep us motivated. There was no guarantee that you could just show up and become a member of the choir. Even if your attendance was perfect during the trial period, if you could not carry a tune and stay in the correct pitch, you were not invited back. During the trial period, you were invited to sit in the first row of pews to observe how the choir performed and behaved on Sundays. I was so excited to be doing this that I forgot to put on my suit jacket, which was a *no-no*, and greatly disappointed my parents on that Sunday. Once past this trial period, you began to participate with the choir at Sunday service, wearing a vestment of a black, robe like garment with a large white collar and fancy tie that the 'choir Mothers' would tie for each of us before service. But not the white cotta. You had to earn this next vestment over time. And by the third week, that's what I had done.

There was a choir initiation that one had to endure toward the end of one's first year as a member. This included being blind-folded and having eggs smashed in your pants, and being ordered by older choir members to perform several silly yet uncomfortable exercises. The hazing *rituals* would be completed by drinking a repugnant drink mixture of everything imaginable topped off with Red Hot Sauce. It was God awful!

At rehearsals, the sopranos were divided into two sides with Mr. Amend at the piano between us. Each side had a leader, a veteran soprano who would pass out and collect the sheet music we sang from, along with keeping the younger members focused. A special trophy was awarded to one side each month to display on their side of the choir room. It represented which side had "won" the most rehearsals during the previous month. Winning a rehearsal meant that your side had no demerits for bad behavior during rehearsal. There were only two ways to have a demerit counted against your side. If you were late without an excuse, your side received one point. The guys from Flushing seemed to be tardy a lot because "the bus was late."

"One point," would be Mr. Amend's response to their singular and repeated reason for being tardy.

And don't *ever* be caught talking at the same time as the choirmaster.

"One point."

Many rehearsals were so good that no points were meted out, ending that rehearsal in a tie.

I became a 'side leader' toward the end of my soprano career. Fortunately, my side did well during that time. My best friend Fat Dog (his real name was Phillip, and someone stuck that name on him because he loved glazed donuts) was leader of the opposing side.

"I, Phillip, as leader of my side, award this trophy to Hank and his side for Best of the Month. We admit being beaten fair and square and will try hard to win it back for next month's award." I know this verse so well because I heard it so often! My side's efforts each month made sure I rarely had to recite it out loud.

Fat Dog and I, who lived a ways away in Rosedale, played a lot of stickball in the P.S. 160 school yard. Sometimes, his brother Jimmy would be there as well. It was like a homecoming for me, a home field advantage, at P.S. 160. We'd meet up with our broom stick for a bat, pink ball (the same one we used in handball at Lincoln Park), and baseball glove. There was a square on the school's wall that represented the strike zone and a fence about eight feet high that divided the inner playground from the outer one. The outer fence was even higher as it abutted the houses that surrounded the school. These fences provided the ground rules for our play. A batted ball caught was an out. A batted ball that bounces before hitting the first fence was a single. Over the first fence a double. Over both fences, a homerun. When pitching, you'd be about 45 feet from the wall. We'd play for what seemed like hours on end, or until our pitching arms gave out.

Fat Dog once literally saved my life. There was a Sunday afternoon youth group (EYC-Episcopal Young Churchmen) that met in the Parish House, which was a half block walk from the church, through the church cemetery. This group of middle and high school male and female students would plan dances, play basketball in the basement, or just hang out. There was always some kind of food that was provided for us and left in the kitchen. The Parish House had a dumb waiter for larger gatherings that would move food and supplies to the basement, or second floor as needed. One afternoon, Fat Dog and I were in the kitchen. I became curious about the dumb waiter, (a remnant and glimpse back to my wandering days in elementary school) opened the door, and put one hand in the center of the platform that moved the supplies up or down. I pushed down too hard, the dumb waiter began to descend pulling me along. Just as my feet went up in the air, Fat Dog grabbed my ankles in the nick of time before I got pinned between the moving dumb waiter and the shaft it ran in.

"How you be?" His signature greeting, he calmly said to my flustered self after pulling me from the slowly descending dumb waiter.

I had my first experience with real money after I joined the Grace Church Choir at age nine. At six years old, I started receiving a weekly allowance from my parents that was twenty-five cents a week. I emptied the trash cans in the house once a week to earn my quarter. The next year, some grocery shopping and walking to pick up the Sunday paper was added to my chores, my allowance doubled to fifty cents. And when walking the dog and cleaning up after Blackie in the backyard was added the following year, I was earning seventy-five cents each week. This was enough to have a good supply of penny-candy on hand, buy a pinky ball for a dime, a bag of Cats-Eye marbles for fifteen cents, or a plastic model to build for thirty cents. I had options!

Grace Church had a boy's/men's choir, and a girls'/womens' choir. But, to the best of my recollection, only the members of the boys'/mens' choir were paid.

I remember that first small brown envelope with six whole dollars inside, my starting salary at nine years old. I had more spending options for my money! Plus, even though I had my bus pass, my mom would give me an additional thirty cents for a round trip bus ride on the Q9, to and from rehearsals. Friday was special. I got fifty-five cents with the extra quarter to buy a slice of pizza and a soda after rehearsal, from a pizza stand just off of Jamaica Avenue, on our way to the Green Line Bus Terminal on Archer Avenue. When Mr. Lee gave the three of us a ride, I'd pocket it all. I started using my bus pass and saving all of what my mom had given to me. When my time in the choir ended, I was making fifteen dollars a month.

Each spring, the combined boys' and girls' choirs, under the direction of Mr. Amend and a friend of his trained in theater, would put on one of Gilbert and Sullivan's operettas. Years later, I'd come to learn that the images, lyrics, and dialogue that permeated the work of Gilbert and Sullivan included stereotypes and misrepresentations about Japanese people, along with an "unremitted sexism" about the role of women.

I earned a leading role as a caddy lover in *"Trial By Jury."* I dressed as a British sailor to be Ralph Rackstraw in *"HMS Pinafore."* I played the half human, half fairy son of *"IOLANTHE."* I put a huge pillow under my costume to portray Pooh-Bah in *"The Mikado."* And I made a grand entrance as the Duke of Plaza Toro in *"The Gondoliers."* All of this musical and on-stage rehearsing (weekday evenings and Saturdays) was in addition to our regular thrice weekly gatherings in the church's basement for choir rehearsal.

Our parents insisted that we maintain an appropriate commitment to our schoolwork throughout our involvement in these church activities. As such, most of us would use some of this choir-show-rehearsal time as a study time when we were not involved with a particular scene or series of scenes. We all attended different schools, had different teachers and had different texts for the same subject. Several, including myself, were in IGC, SP or Honors classes. Studying together was a natural thing to do as our academic goals were to do more than *get over - that is to say, doing just enough to pass.* On occasions I remember both myself and others, with our New York State Regents Prep books, studying together when we had a break or were not on stage during a choir show rehearsal. This kind of strong side and likeminded networking became the guardrail against any potential weak side networking; those things that are not in support of our shared academic goals. The outcome of having successful lives and careers for ourselves was front and center.

This is what our parents insisted we do. Most of my friends who shared these times with me have gone on to find success in their lives and careers. Judges. Lawyers. Financiers. Doctors. Psychologists. Business owners. Teachers. The attitude that permeated our relationships was "nobody wins unless everybody wins," was ever present.

I stand firm in my belief that a major reason that I have found success, health, and happiness in my personal and professional lives, has a strong root in these early experiences in the choir shows, where public speaking was involved. As an *anti-racist educator,* my classroom is my stage, and my students/attendees are a captive audience for me to pay-it-forward to *a time I may not see.*

In addition to rehearsal rules and expectations, Mr. Amend had rules we needed to follow outside of rehearsal time. One was not to eat any candy or anything sweet prior to any rehearsal or service. *Doing so would coat your throat with sugar,* he'd tell us, and not allow you to sing with the same clarity. He was right. Your range decreased and the sound was different from that of the sound of bouncing off the roof of your mouth, we had been trained to do.

Another rule was that we should not be playing football, basketball, or anything that requires physical exertion before rehearsal. You needed to have control of your breathing he would remind us. But, on occasion, there we were, five minutes before the 4:30 P.M Tuesday start time, out in the grass in a yet unused area of the church cemetery playing tackle football and eating Sugar Babies. We'd sprint back to the basement choir room to get to our seats before Mr. Amend played the first chord on the piano to begin rehearsal.

If you appeared out of breath, he'd call out, "One point!" accompanied by the stare of death rivaled only by the one your mom can give.

If you couldn't sing the first warm up exercise, "One point!" this time rivaled only by the stare of death your dad can give.

In all those yesterdays and more while in the choir, we were almost angels.

107-35-139TH STREET, JAMAICA, NEW YORK 11435

I've grown to realize how privileged and blessed I was growing up. Both parents are present and living in a single-family home. Today, some young people as they are growing up are often forced to move yearly, bi-annually, or even monthly, to a new residence. The needs of these children, for reasons they had no control over, were not met by their parents. I was fortunate to be able to grow up in a stable, caring, loving environment that included my grandmother, my mom's mom. That was the home base of my village.

There was also a lot of positive networking and watching out for each other's backs amongst my neighborhood peers in my formative years. And there were a lot of us, girls and boys, all within three to five years in age of each other. Friends one day, enemies the next, then friends again.

Benny. Nancy. Charles. Don. Clyde. Pixie. Janine. Effie. Jean. Carol. Ralph. Michael. Carmen. Deborah. Craig. Freddy. Eugene. Ronald. Jerry. Peter. Donna. Yvette.

Our little corner of paradise on 139th Street in Jamaica, Queens was a tree lined cul-de-sac of single-family homes. Every Labor Day, the local civic organization would sponsor and arrange for a day-long Block Party, that was a blast from sunrise to sunset. Two policemen would be hired, and they'd put barricades at the street intersection with 109th Avenue so no traffic could enter the block. All the adults would put their cars in their garages to clear the street. The fun began at 9:00 AM.

Several barbeque grills lined the curbside with hot dogs, hamburgers, corn-on-the-cob, chicken, and hot sausages. Other stations had tables to keep the potato and macaroni salad cool. Still other places were trash barrels full of beverages; one for the kids, another for the adult beverages.

Music filled the air.

Games were played all day with prizes for everyone.

Running races were held for the children by age and gender. Benny would always win my age group. He was so fast that he'd seem to get to the finish line before most of us could get started.

There was a raffle drawing toward the end of the day for a grand prize of a brand-new bicycle for one lucky child. I would always. "do anything you ask, Lord," if I could just win that bike. Alas, I never did. But as I shared previously my parents made sure that I did have a bike to ride.

As dusk arrived, it was the adults' turn to dance in the streets to the sounds of big band and calypso music.

139th Street ran parallel to the Van Wyck Expressway. This is a major thoroughfare from the international airport (Idlewild, then renamed Kennedy) to Manhattan. Residing about two miles from there resulted in a constant sound of aircraft landing. There was a service road along the expressway for local traffic, then about 50 feet of grass until you got to the three lanes of the highway. This proximity to our homes gave us the opportunity to see important world leaders as their motorcade made its way to Manhattan. Presidents Einsenhower and Kennedy were frequent visitors and seeing Pope John XXIII was a once in a lifetime opportunity. But when Nikita Krushev came to speak at the United Nations, we couldn't leave our block, and no one from anywhere else was allowed within one block of the Van Wyck.

There was another constant sound from above. New York Airways ran a helicopter shuttle between downtown Manhattan and the three metropolitan airports - Idlewild, LaGuardia and Newark, New Jersey. One afternoon while a group of us played double dutch jump rope on the street, we heard the sound of a helicopter's engines sputtering and about to stall out. As I looked up to see the impending disaster overhead, parents, too, came running out of their homes to see what was almost overhead. Mrs. Strider, Jean's mom, knelt in the middle of 139th Street and prayed out loud "Please don't land on my house," over and over and over. The pilot managed to safely land the aircraft, on the service road, with minimum damage to anyone's property.

Remember Ajax Park, where we'd play tackle football? One school day afternoon, another New York Airways helicopter had to set down on the ball field after experiencing engine trouble.

As I said, there were a lot of us. Finding someone to play with was never a problem. Whether it was punch ball, going to Ajax, Lincoln or Sunnyside park, there was always something to do and someone to do it with. Other than watching the television. Which only offered seven channels in the NYC area: 2 (CBS), 4 (NBC), 5 (local station WNEW), 7 (ABC), 9 (local station WWOR), 11 (local station WPIX), 13 (educational channel).

I learned how to bowl (ten pin) during these times. I'd join Craig and Charles on Saturday mornings to go to a local bowling alley where a neighborhood woman had organized a Bantam League for us. There were fifteen or so others who were not from our cul-de-sac, and Mrs. Brunson mixed us all up to form teams of three. There were three games you'd play against an opponent and after three games, the total number of pins amassed by the team of three would win. My average was about 145, and one incredible day I rolled a 196 to earn a Bantam patch for the "175 Club." Not too long ago, in my retirement, I went back to this form of exercise for a couple of years. And rolled multiple games over 200, including 226. *Still got it.*

There were also Saturday theatrical performances for school aged children at the Lowes and RKO Alden theaters on Jamaica Avenue. I don't know how my parents got me tickets, but seeing these live onstage was a boost of confidence for me. I'd envision myself in the role, facing the audience, picking up on the mannerisms of the actors, and calling on these visions when on stage during our choir shows.

The Christmas season was a special time at everyone's house in the neighborhood. There always seemed to be snow around on the big day, and the adults would try to outdo each other with outdoor lights and decorations. Maybe it was one-ups-man ship or community pride and involvement, but most every home in our area was adorned with lights decorating their home's landscape. From my bedroom window, I'd scan the night skies on December 24th hoping for a glimpse of you-know-who. I remember when the bubble called Santa Claus popped for me.

It was a Sunday evening. I was eight and it was less than a week before December 25th. We just finished dinner. Family time around the dinner table was expected and a part of my life growing up. Dad was lying down in one of the two second-floor bedrooms after dinner, Granny (my mom's mom) who lived with us, was in the other second floor bedroom crocheting. The bathroom was between the two bedrooms. Granny, who was born in 1875, lived to be 105. She once told me of the *Blizzard of* 1888 and the snow piled up covering the windows of homes.

Mom was cleaning the kitchen after the Sunday meal. I was playing in my attic bedroom on the third floor with our dog Blackie, a little black terrier. I came down from the attic to sit on the top of the stairs that led to the living room. This was my perch on December 24th to see Jolly Old St. Nick, but I'd always fall asleep and wake up in bed, carried there by my dad, on Christmas morning.

Blackie went into Granny's room. I got on my stomach to crawl after him. As I did, I saw under Granny's bed a huge box that read OPERATION MOONBASE, the number one item on my list to Santa. As my eyes saw what I wasn't supposed to see, Granny simultaneously called out in a stern voice to my mother, "Mary, call Hank and give him a glass of water for me." I was immediately summoned to the kitchen by my mom. I guess Granny hustled to rouse my dad and have him move the present to some other secluded spot. When I came back to Granny's room with the water, all that was under the bed was dust.

I was born at 7:17 PM, but not 7:17 PM last night.

SUMMERTIME

*J*uly and August for me often included going to the Central Queens YMCA Day Camp on Parsons Boulevard. The 'Y' was caddy-corner from the Grace Church Parish House, so I was familiar with the area. When I think back to those times, I remember the organization of the camp's groupings mirrored those of the Military Academy at West Point.

My dad served in the Army during World War II. He was the interpreter for the Company and he often talked about being a part of the force that landed on on the beaches of Normandy, France on June 7, 1944, D-Day+1. We'd watch *The Longest Day* and *Battle of the Bulge* together and he'd encourage me to "Watch the tv, you might see me." I still have the dictionary he carried with him when he came ashore. Recently, I was leading a multi-day professional development for educators and shared this story. The next day, one of the attendees gifted me a small bottle of sand that he had collected on a trip to the same beaches at Normandy just a few years earlier. His gesture touched my heart.

Of course, the images in those and other World War II movies did not, at that time, include the contributions of Black, Latinx, Native American, and women to the war effort. Dad would often call out cadence whenever the story showed men in training. Sometimes he'd stand upright in our living room and holler, "To the left. To the left,

To the left, right, left. To the rear march!" He still had his combat boots, and one winter my feet finally fit into them.

Beginning around age seven, I was assigned to the youngest group, Prep A. A few years later, I moved up to Prep B. The two oldest groups were the Plebes and Cadets. I never got to the top two groups at day camp. But this disappointment was not as severe as missing out on being Captain of the Crossing Guards. When I got to Prep B, my friend Ronald was already in the Plebes and Cadets group, and his older brother was a counselor for one of those grownup groups. Maybe there was some kind of karma going on to pay attention to.

During each week, two groups (Prep A and B) would stay at the 'Y' for a "building day" that included swimming lessons, arts and crafts (I could never master any of the different stitches required to make a lanyard, but made a mean ashtray), game room time after lunch with billiards, and even an ice-cream machine if you had the change required. Some of us would head out after lunch with two of the counselors and walk fifteen minutes to a nearby playground for a

softball game. By this time, I had become a big fan of baseball and prided myself on knowing not only the rules of the game, but how to keep score as well. When I was 10, I hit twelve home runs, tied with another camper named Chuck, and we were each awarded a (three inch) trophy. I still have mine today. Then we'd retrace our steps back to the 'Y' and to the pool for an afternoon free swim.

There were the day trips, many times to a beach or state park within an hour's ride of the 'Y.' The yellow school buses would be all in line on the side street and after morning attendance and check in, where our destination would be announced, and we'd find out what number bus to board when we left the meeting area in the 'Y's' main gymnasium.

Yellow school buses have no air conditioning, so the windows were immediately lowered as we found our seat for the ride to Riis Beach, which always had a lot of seashells on the beach. Or Sunken Meadow State Park and Beach, when the tide was out one could safely venture over 100 yards from the shore. Or Heckscher State Park and Beach, which had the best hot dogs, second only to Needicks on Jamaica Avenue. Or a day at Rye Beach Amusement Park. As much fun as the ride to one of these places was, the ride back was often filled with the songs from the Top 10 of the time on local radio stations.

But as the bus turned onto Parsons Boulevard for the final three blocks to the 'Y,' we'd begin, "We're from the 'Y.' And nobody can deny. And if you can not hear us. We'll shout a little louder!" With all the windows down, the boisterous rhythmic refrain grew louder as it was repeated by campers and counselors alike, until the bus came to a stop for us to disembark and join our parents who were there awaiting our arrival. They heard us too! The bus driver never seemed to mind our youthful enthusiasm. He just wanted to get us back safely.

I had just finished the 6th grade when my summers got even better. As the second half of August began, and day camp ended, my parents sent me for a week of sleep-away camp. I guess I must have told them I liked it because the following summer got 'better-er.'

After the first four weeks of summer going to the 'Y's' Day Camp, the next four weeks, my parents were able to send me to YMCA

Camp Brooklyn. This was a sleep-away camp for boys nestled in the Pocono Mountains in Paupack, Pike County, Pennsylvania. It was about ninety minutes from Queens and fifteen minutes from the man-made Lake Wallenpaupack. This would be my longest time away from home for an extended period of time, until the next year when my parents were able to send me for the entire eight weeks that Camp Brooklyn operated in the summer months. I'd leave after the 4th of July and return home eight weeks later. It certainly was quite different from the one-night sleepovers we'd have back on 139th Street.

Camp Brooklyn was where I learned to water ski. The swimming lessons I had received during Day Camp paid dividends as you were required to swim several laps of the camp's swimming area, to earn the chance to learn to ski. And I met the requirements. After being fitted with the right size life preserver by the spotter in the boat, the instructor taught us how to do several water starts. When I figured out my balance, I did all of these starts, and then began confidently crossing the boat wake or being on 'the whip.' Going really fast, almost perpendicular to the 60-horsepower boat. I did fall on the whip once, and it was the most joyous time bouncing across the lake's surface like a skipping rock, until I came to a safe stop and was picked up.

In some ways, the military influence at Camp Brooklyn compared to that of Day Camp at the 'Y.' Using a PA system with speakers throughout the camp, we'd hear a recording of 'reveille' trumpeted to wake us up. Another 'military signal' for table waiters to scurry to the mess hall and set their respective tables for the meal. And yet another bugle recording to 'flag raising' meant that you had to stop whatever you were doing, and place your hand over your heart. Then at 8 AM, as we walked from our cabins to the dining hall, the bugle recording played "Come and get your chow!".

The waiter and mealtime calls were repeated for the lunchtime, which followed the morning's activities. Part of the mornings included swimming lessons. Softball. Tennis. Archery. Basketball. Riflery. Canoeing. Row boating. Sailing. Arts and Crafts. Hiking. There was a rotation as the week progressed, both by day, age group, and morning vs. afternoon, but swim lessons and softball seemed to be a part of each day for me.

The youngest campers were the Cherokee, and they had the furthest to walk to the dining hall. The middle group was the Iroquois. And the oldest group of campers were the Apache, who had the shortest distance to walk to the dining hall.

On the other hand, the Cherokee were closest to Paradise (the bathrooms and shower areas), while the Apache, had the furthest to go. I was an Apache and over the ensuing summers would go from Cabin 7 to Cabin 1. We never really learned anything about these Indigenous names, nor their cultures over the time I went to Camp Brooklyn.

Everyone looked forward to receiving mail from home or friends after lunch. My mom, who had immaculate Palmer Method handwriting, made sure I got at least two letters each week. And I had a 'girlfriend' who would send letters in envelopes that had the sweet smell of perfume. There was a tradition that if you received more than one piece of mail that day, you had to "Sing-For-Your-Mail" in front of the entire camp. I had to do this a couple of times, especially when I'd get a perfume-laced letter, and my choir days and singing lessons helped a lot. Fortunately, though, I never had to do so by myself, as was the case for a few others who would get three, four or even five letters on a given day when no one else had gotten more than one.

Our after-lunch time began with an hour or so rest period where you were expected to remain in your cabin and do just that—rest.

One counselor and no more than seven campers in each cabin provided our board. What followed was a potpourri of choices for the remaining afternoon time. And there was always about a forty-five minute free swim before dinner. You had to have a buddy and make use of the 'buddy-board' for checking into a specific part of the dock area. During free swim, there would be a 'buddy check' called by the counselors. Find your buddy and raise a hand together while the counselors counted and verified the number on the board with the number of buddies in that area. It was smooth and ran like clockwork whenever called.

On occasion, a 'Lost-Man Drill' would be practiced with the sounding of a huge bell which hung from the lifeguard tower. When the bell sounded, wherever you were in camp, you were to return to your cabin ASAP for attendance, while a designated group of staff searched the water for the person in distress. The expectations were like that of a fire drill in school.

As free swim ended and we walked back to our cabins, I'd notice several campers of varying ages walking extra fast or even running back to their cabin. They knew that the next bugle would be for 'waiters' to come to the dining hall for set up, and time was not on their side. Soon thereafter, as I was changing from my swim trunks to dry clothes, we'd hear that 'military bugle' summoning waiters to their assigned task. Whenever I was a waiter, I looked forward to it because no one at the table could eat until the waiter got back from the kitchen and had served their portion. A little perk like being in the Crossing Guards.

Just as in the morning, before the call to dinner, there was 'flag lowering' where again, the expectation was to stop whatever you were doing. If outside, you'd face in the direction of the flag, hand over your heart. Using the camp "store" came after dinner. My parents had put ten dollars in my account, and we were given a card to be punched after any purchase. It was like going to the corner store back home, but only once a day. It was rare that someone had nothing in their account. After a short rest in our cabins, there'd be an evening activity for each group that often involved a campfire and some kind of scary story. I don't know what they were thinking, but that's not the best way to put kids to rest at night.

One of my favorite songs that we sang at the end of evening activity, was by the artists Peter, Paul, and Mary. The words were:

"If I had a hammer, I'd hammer in the morning, I'd hammer in the evening, all over this land. I'd hammer out danger. I'd hammer out a warning. I'd hammer out love between my brothers and my sisters, all over the land. Oooo-Ooo-Oo

If I had a bell I'd ring it in the morning, I'd ring it in the evening, all over this land. I'd ring out danger, I'd ring out warning. I'd ring out love between my brothers and my sisters, all over this land. Oooo-Ooo-Oo

If I had a song, I'd sing it in the morning, I'd sing it in the evening, all over this land. I'd sing out danger. I'd sing out the warning. I'd sing out the love between my brothers and my sisters, all over this land. Oooo-Ooo-Oo

Now I've got a hammer and I've got a bell, and I've got a song to sing all over this land. It's the hammer of justice. It's the bell of freedom. It's a song about love between my brothers and sisters, all over this land."

Some songs don't have a shelf life and span the decades and events of time. This remains one such song from my yesterdays.

Then, to the tune of taps, we'd all sing these words, "Day is done. Gone, the sun. From the hills to the lakes to the skies. All is well, safely rest. God is nigh." Everyone would head back to their cabins where we'd hear the bugle again, sounding taps over the PA system to end the day as we placed our heads down for the night.

We all looked forward to the Special Event Days at Camp Brooklyn. I know I did. They were always around a theme and the camp was divided up into four teams with equal numbers of Cherokee, Iroquois and Apache on each team for competitions held over the course of multiple days. The event would usually begin after the evening meal and brought out different degrees of lavish decoration, displayed by each team in an opening ceremony where they would present a skit, a song, and a team plaque that would be displayed in the dining hall. Each teams performance would was judged by some members of the senior staff, including the Camp Director, Assistant Director, and Waterfront Director. The event's first points were awarded after all the teams had given their presentation. The 'games' included various alterations to different activities we were familiar with, and some that were strictly athletic.

One of the summers when I was at Camp Brooklyn, the theme was Space Days, a reflection of the country's efforts in the national goal to land a man on the moon. It was during Space Days that I first uncovered my developing talents as a runner. The event, a one to two mile run, was held as the opening race and the entire camp was assembled on the baseball field. The course was a little less than a mile up a mountainside. All the runners were familiar with the path as we had previously traversed it on a hike a few times. There, we'd find a staff member who gave us some kind of small object to carry with us back to the finish line, which was, literally, stepping on home plate of the baseball field to finish. I remember that there was a camper named Fred, whom everyone knew was a member of his school's cross-country team. He bolted to the front as the race began. He was several yards in front of me, but I never lost sight of him as we ran uphill. Even after reaching the top and beginning the run back down, I didn't seem to be making up any ground on Fred, even though there were still others climbing as we were headed back down. When he emerged from the forest toward the bottom, I had gotten closer. It was about 250 yards from home plate when I used the momentum of the last part of the hill to gain even more ground. As we raced across the field, I got closer and as we approached home plate, I triumphantly took the final step onto home plate, less than a stride ahead of Fred. Everyone was cheering and applauding the efforts of all the runners, some of whom were a few minutes behind. But the best was yet to come.

At the end of the summer, the last five days before we left for home were the annual Olympic Games. And that's exactly what they were. Just as for Space Days, the camp was divided up into four teams with equal numbers of Cherokee, Iroquois and Apache on each team. There were running races, tennis matches, basketball games, archery, riflery, softball throw, arts and crafts creations that were judged, swimming, sailing, canoe, and rowboat races. On the last day, the counselors on each team participated in a 'greased watermelon' water polo game.

For the 1966 Camp Brooklyn Olympic Games, I was on a team named The Salonikans. The name comes from the second largest city in Greece on the Aegean Sea, Thessaloniki. To the tune of God Bless America, our song included the refrain "Salonika. Salonika. God shed His grace on thee. And crown our best in all contests with sweeping victory!" And over the ensuing five days of the Olympics, the Solonikans were triumphant!

The Games began following the evening meal with the Opening Ceremonies. Here, as at Space Day, each team presented their skit, song and cheer to be judged. Then, the Marathon was the opening event. It was about a two to three mile run, aptly called "Around the Lake Run." I would be one of the runners representing Salonika. Again, my main competition was Fred. But this time, I immediately dashed to the front following a counselor who would lead the way. No one else was close when I looked back as I crossed the finish line some twenty or so minutes later. When all the runners finished, an honor given to the winner of the Marathon each year was to light the Olympic torch that glowed day and night throughout the Olympics, outside of the dining hall. I climbed the three steps to ignite the torch. Yesterday.

The Apache Salonikans held their own against the competition over the five days. But it was the Iroquois and especially the Cherokee members of Solonika that provided the winning margin. On the last evening, there was a closing ceremony, that was judged for the final points to be awarded. And an award was given to the outstanding athlete in each of the three age groups. I still have mine.

I continued attending Camp Brooklyn (still in the Apache) until I reached my last year of high school, when I was invited to apply for the C.I.T. (Counselors in Training) Program. The best way to describe C.I.T. would be that we were both trainee and camper, in the roles that we fulfilled. There was helping with the arts and crafts program, monitoring the 'buddy-board' and helping with swimming lessons for the Cherokee, carrying the equipment to the fields for softball, archery, basketball or riflery. We had our own cabin, named Seneca, set away from the rest of the campers and right along the lake.

One day in early July, I was assigned to be the assistant for the instructor/counselor in charge of archery during the Iroquois activity time. Although safety was first and foremost, there were times when the limits of this were, shall I say, stretched. Just like safety was stretched riding our bikes out onto the runways at JFK Airport.

Each of us had our own bow, quiver, and several arrows. But instead of aiming at the targets that stood about twenty-five yards away, the counselor had our group form a circle in the forest opening. I had done this before, so I knew what was coming. We'd each take an arrow, string it for release, turn our aim to straight up in the air, aiming for the sky above. On the count of three, everyone released their arrow high into the sky before scattering into the nearby woods as the arrows landed harmlessly where we'd been standing only moments before.

Everyone had their bow and one arrow.

A circle was formed.

We instructed the campers on what we were about to do.

The counselor began the countdown.

"Three. Two. One. Release."

Everything went in slow motion, for at the very moment we released our arrows into the sky, the "Lost-Man Drill" bell sounded. DING-DING-DING. Pause. DING-DING-DING. Pause. DING-DING-DING. As previously described, this meant that everyone had to run and return to their cabin ASAP—while the arrows were still in the air! It was most fortunate that no one was struck by a descending arrow because, as you might imagine, the aim of some in the group changed with the sounding of the bell, to arcing them in different directions, including the route back to the cabin area.

To make matters worse, as we got to the road crossing that led back to the cabins, about seventy-five yards away on the road, at the top of a hill where the Pike County Post Office was located, a momma bear and two of her cubs were also crossing the road. It seemed that the first thought of the younger campers seemed to be "Oh wow. A bear. Let's get closer to see." However, counselors and C.I.Ts sternly directed the crowd of about fifty campers away from the animals to be sure that they did not get closer for a better look. Fortunately, the momma bear and her cubs headed off into the woods behind camp, and we were able to herd the campers in the right direction, back to their cabins.

Later that month, we listened over the radio in our cabin on July 20, 1969, to hear the famous words, "One small step for man. One giant leap for mankind," spoken by Neil Armstrong. I'd describe myself as a bit of a space-geek growing up. I followed the success and failures of three NASA programs. Beginning with Mercury, followed by Gemini, and now Apollo.

It was also the summer of the Woodstock Music Festival, held in August. Some of the counselors wanted to go, but camp wasn't over yet. A few did manage to finagle about 36 hours over a couple of days to take the one hour trip to Sullivan County in New York State.

It was also the Summer of Soul in New York City, an event that was hardly known until recently, unless you were *there*, in the city in the summer of 1969. I wasn't, and so learning about this event *years* later came as a shock. Not only had I missed it, but also missed knowing about it.

Organized by the Harlem Cultural Festival, the event was held in Mount Morris Park for six consecutive Sundays, beginning on June 29th. Among the many performers over those six weeks were Nina Simone, Stevie Wonder, the 5th Dimension, Gladys Knight and the

Pips, Sly and the Family Stone, BB King, Hugh Masekela, Mahalia Jackson, and Mavis Staples. The festival was an opportunity for the community of Harlem to come together at the end of a decade of grief and loss of leaders, such as Martin Luther King Jr., MalcolmX, and Medgar Evers.

History that is lost, stolen, or strayed is no longer new to me from those yesterdays. That is why it is important for me to pay-it-forward with the stories, such as The Summer of Soul, that push back against a negative stereotype toward those who identify as being of the global majority. We, who are Black, Brown, Native/Indigenous, Asian American, Pacific Islander, Multi/Bi-racial, bring value and humanity to the full-telling of American History.

The C.I.T. canoe trip along the Delaware River, beginning from Port Jervis, New York and ending back in Pennsylvania, took place toward the end of the camping season. I learned how to paddle a canoe, do a cross-bow-rudder while sitting in the canoe's bow seat, steer the canoe from the stern seat, swamp a canoe, and rescue a swamped canoe, all in preparation for this trip. These skills came in quite handy during our four-day voyage, and I also learned how to water-proof my sleeping bag and belongings that I'd be taking along with me. This waterproofing skill *really* came in handy in a big way.

We'd have breakfast and then get in our canoes and start paddling around 9 AM and would go for a couple hours. Then we'd stop along the banks of the river to rest and snack, before setting out again for another couple of hours. We'd have lunch, rest, then head out one last time for the day to our campsite for the night. It was beautiful weather. The river was calm and looked like a pane of glass, and there was a gentle breeze at our backs, along with the slow current. As a freight train passed our fleet of seven canoes, the engineer honored the lifelong request made of them, especially by kids, to sound the horn of the engine. The blast sequence lasted less than ten seconds, but we all felt like this was the greatest-thing-since-sliced-bread as the train passed by going in the opposite direction from us, along the tracks on the shores of the river.

On the second day, everyone was looking forward, with a certain degree of trepidation, to the most challenging part of our trip. I remember hearing that the part of the river we would be entering had the name "Gap" in it, and that this would include navigating whitewater. The two staff members accompanying us had been preparing us right up to this day with the warning to "Stay to the left," as each canoe would begin its bumpy and wet ride down the fifty to seventy-five yards of fast moving water.

I was paddling in the stern the previous day, and Erik was in the bow. I'd been canoeing with him at camp. I felt fine when I said "Okay" to him, asking to start the day in the stern.

Our backpacks were fitted securely between the two bars inside of the canoe.

As we neared the rapids, I heard one last time from the group leaders, "Stay to the left!" I don't know why, but Erik was having difficulty guiding us to the left as the current suddenly increased. I finally shouted out, "Erik, stay to the left!"

Our canoe headed down the right side of the rapids, bouncing up, down then over the side we went as our canoe swamped. Our backpacks? They were both moving down the river ahead of us, but floating, thank goodness. We hadn't tied each to the bars inside the canoe, so one of the canoes ahead of us corralled our packs, then did a canoe-over-canoe rescue to right our vessel. Before getting back in, I told Erik to switch places with me, and I'd be in the stern steering our canoe for the duration of the trip. He didn't argue

SP CLASS

The summer before I entered junior high school in 1964, was a tumultuous one in New York City. The controversy was over bussing to promote racial integration in the city's school population. One of the epicenters where this controversy erupted and overflowed was J.H.S. 109 in Queens Village. Reporting by the New York Times then stated that, "a few years ago the school was a controversial symbol of the Board of Education's efforts to promote racial integration." The Times report went on to say that the board was now under criticism for "encouraging racial imbalance." Feeder schools that were predominantly upper middle class, white, and Jewish would no longer be guaranteed to be assigned to 109. And folks who looked like me would now be assigned to the school. A series of angry confrontations occurred in the summer months that resulted in my parents receiving a letter in early August, stating that instead of attending J.H.S.109 as I was originally assigned under the desegregation plan, I would be attending J.H.S.119 in the Glendale section of Queens, where it borders Brooklyn. One other classmate (Mary-Jean) from my IGC cohort was also assigned to 119 under this revised plan.

Regardless of which school I would attend, a perk for me was that I could travel on the Q40 each morning with my mom. She'd pay 15 cents, but I only paid a nickel, which was the fare for junior/

senior high students using their bus pass. Drop your nickel in the box, show your pass, and find a seat. But because of my reassignment, I'd be taking the bus, a train, and then a city bus each morning to get to school. My mom and I headed out for the three block walk from home to the Q40 bus stop on Lakewood Avenue and 142nd Street. We'd be taking this same walk together for the foreseeable future. The bus ride began going down Lakewood Avenue and taking a left onto Sutphin Boulevard. We'd get off together at the corner of Jamaica Avenue and Sutphin Boulevard to climb the steps to the train platform. Sometimes my mom would go to the other platform. There were only two stops in that direction, and she would board that train first as she wanted to be sure she got a seat for her lengthy ride into lower Manhattan. Smart lady, my mom was.

When I left P.S.123, there were 25-27 students in our class. Of that number, there were two white students. When I arrived for the first day at homeroom in 7SP (Special Progress) at J.H.S. 119, there were 25-27 students—Mary-Jean and I, along with a Japanese boy named Glen, were the only students of color in the class. I was about to be challenged academically like never before, as the passing grade in the major SP classes was 85% or B+.

The educational concept and approach to learning in those times was guided by academic tracking. This became particularly evident to me as I began junior high school. There were as many as fifteen classes at each of the three grade levels, 7th, 8th, 9th at J.H.S. 119. As I found out, the number after your academic grade/year spoke volumes about the expected academic potential for that group.

For example, 7SP, 7-1 and 7-2 could at least *see* college in their future. But those in 7-12, 7-13, and 7-14 I'm sure could also see the writing on the wall for their future, because of the lack of expectations directed their way. Whenever I reminisce about my junior high years, I find myself reflecting on how the academic lives and future outcomes/careers unfolded, not only for those tracked with more challenging curriculum, but for those with far less challenge who were predominantly kids of color like me.

My two years in junior high would present the first fork in my life's road. I say two years because in 7SP we did the entire seventh and eighth grade curriculums between September and June of 7th grade. The following September would find us all in the 9th grade, having 'skipped' 8th grade. When sharing this part of my story with middle and high school students, I sometimes ask them to tell me what it's like to be in the eighth grade, as I never had the experience. "What do you want me to know about 8th grade?", I'll ask. They'll share about how small the sixth-graders look, or something about the food in the cafeteria, or school dances, or even a teacher that they remember.

For the first time, I was introduced to a departmentalized schedule, going to different teachers for each subject. My seventh-grade homeroom teacher was Mrs. Rohm, a slim-in-stature woman who was near retirement age, she always smelled like cigarette smoke. She also happened to be our math teacher. Her approach to teaching the combined seventh and eighth grade curriculum was, "here it is, you'd better get it, because I won't repeat it." Apparently, there was no time for redundancy in 7SP. In English class we read Julius Caesar and other than, "Et tu Brute?" I honestly don't remember much else except that reading and understanding Shakespeare was unnecessarily hard.

Considering my daily travel schedule to school on public transportation, it was no small task to maintain that B+ average across the board. Add on going directly home each afternoon before heading back out to choir rehearsal on Tuesdays and Wednesdays, finding time to study was at a premium. But I achieved and exceeded the expectation throughout seventh grade. My dad, going back to those lunchtime sessions in early elementary school, always reminded me to do more than is expected of you to get ahead. Hidden in that message was that as a black child, I had to do twice as much to keep up and stay ahead. I've tried to maintain that practice from school to the athletic field and in my personal life, to this day.

While at 119, I had a few interactions with students that reflected on what the research of Fordham and Ogbu identifies as "the burden of acting white." Their research, done in the 1980s, brought light to an ongoing conversation in public schools in understanding one of the factors impacting the achievement of Black students. They defined this burden as "any behavior that fell within a white cultural frame of reference." At this time, in my schooling, learning the school curriculum and meeting or surpassing the accompanying academic standard was viewed by some people as "acting white." Rarely as it was, there were the looks of disdain directed my way by other black students. Looks that said, "What are you doing in SP getting good grades?" Ironically, I also had the rare occasion to receive similar looks and feel the same disdain from white classmates and white teachers that said, "What are you doing here in SP getting good grades?" Although cordially intended, I often felt like I was on the outside looking in.

The following September, at the beginning of ninth grade, I had, for the first time, a male teacher for an academic subject. Mr. Henry Gruen was my homeroom and social studies teacher, and a refreshing change from the stuffy Mrs. Rohm. He was a young, energetic gentleman who knew how to light the fire and bellow at just the right time. It was, again, like the 'reality pedagogy' I previously referenced. Having the same first name as my teacher was as good as being a Crossing Guard.

We all subscribed to the New York Times, which was delivered daily in bulk to our classroom where we began with reading the paper during homeroom. Mr. Gruen would have a section for us to read that was connected to the day's lesson to review, but students would also initiate some conversation about other topics of interest from the paper. For example, conversations about current events turned from just giving factual information by rote, into spontaneous interactions about the civil rights legislation, or the pros and cons of the space program, or the unfolding Vietnam War.

I still loved baseball and was quite disappointed when not selected for the school's softball team in the seventh grade. I thought I did more than asked on the asphalt field during tryouts. Hit the ball hard.

Field my infield position flawlessly. Handled the drills and ran as well as others. But maybe it was because I was only in the seventh grade, and the final team was rostered with almost exclusively ninth graders. I went to watch one game and observed this, but also observed that there was no one on the field or bench who looked like me. You know what I'm saying? There were no black kids or kids of color on that team.

The following year when I got to ninth grade, I decided to try out for the basketball team. Didn't make that one either, but there were kids on the roster who looked like me. I approached the coach and became the team's scorekeeper at our games. I felt like a part of something in a similar way to how I felt about being a member of the choir. I set, at the time, a school record of over 600 sit-ups completed during a given amount of time in PE class. The pain and weird feelings in my stomach muscles for the remainder of that day were no joke as I sat in my afternoon classes.  During the spring of ninth grade, I tried out for a sport that I would years later excel at, and one that there were no tryouts for. The track team. My event was the 880 yard or half mile run and I was successful, getting better with each competition. I recorded a 2:35 PR for the event and earned my "G" varsity letter.

There were two city wide public transit strikes in the two years I attended 119. Nonetheless, schools were still open each day. My dad, who worked nights and was home in the mornings, would drive me to school. Mr. Milan, Craig's dad from the neighborhood, would pick me up at school and bring me safely home.

I got to buy my lunch every day in junior high, but not from the school cafeteria. There was a popular deli at the bus stop where I got off the city bus, one block from school, where lots of us bought our lunch before trudging the final block to the school's entrance. My favorite order was a ham and Swiss cheese hero sandwich, mustard on the bread, lettuce, tomatoes, a Hawaiian Punch, and a bag of chips. I was good to go!

At the end of the ninth grade, I took my first statewide regents exam. This one for algebra. Taking the regents exam throughout New York State was an annoying rite of passage that students had to endure at each year's end in different subjects. I had been assigned to I.G.C. for three years and had now completed the junior high special progress program in <u>two</u> years. As I prepared for the exam, I was believing that the reason for my success in school *must* be something that I was born with. I thought that I had "it." Mrs. Kelly told me so back in second grade. I had bought into the American model of development that said some people are born smart, and others never will be. This misguided belief about the attribution for my academic success up to this point resulted in my preparation not being what it should have been, and I produced a 59% on that algebra regents exam. My parents didn't like that. In the following three years of high school, I woke up to realize that the reason for my success and "getting good grades" had everything to do with the effective effort that I was making. And had very little, if at all, to do with what I was born with. My parents and family, Mr. Amend, Mrs. Kelly, Miss Shepherd, Mr. Gruen, neighborhood parents and my peers had shaped a culture that would give me confidence in taking realistic and challenging academic risks. Success was not guaranteed. But the combination of thinking I can, and making an effective effort would put me in a great position to learn. To this day, I practice this process of development, and hold the belief that learning is demonstrated best by a change in behavior.

THE LIONS OF RICHMOND HILL

After catching the Q40 each morning to the Sutphin Boulevard stop of the EL, I'd now be traveling one additional stop on the EL to 111th Street station, make my way down the stairs for the one block walk down 113th Street to find Richmond Hill High School. Home of the Lions and where I'd be spending my school time for the next three years.

I entered through a series of doorways and into a grand foyer with a spiral staircase that ascended on the far wall from the entrance. The auditorium doors were to the right and the gymnasium entrance doors to the left. Students of varying racial and socioeconomic backgrounds were standing around in small groups, conversing with each other. I saw a few of my SP classmates in a similar posture to mine. It went through my mind and perhaps theirs too, that we were the youngest (I had become fourteen in April) in this mass of humanity. And I could easily tell who the first-year students at The Hill were; like me, standing by ourselves, who didn't know anybody.

As the bell rang, suddenly there appeared several of the oldest students, the seniors, who brought comfort to me and I'm sure others in the assembled group waiting to start the day. I heard some of the seniors say to others, "Can I help you?" Or "Let me show you the way." Adjusting to this new environment was off to a good start.

One of the first classes I went to on that first day of 10th grade was geometry. It was here that I met Mr. Paternoster. A short, younger man, with black hair and rimmed glasses, and a wry kind of smile that was somewhat like that of a predator trying to gain your favor before pouncing. As he introduced himself, he told us a little about the origins of his name; his family ancestral line was Italian, and "pater" in Italian means *father*. He tried to assure us that he'd treat us as his own children, but in the next sentence wrote on the blackboard the day and time that the algebra regents exam would be given. He did treat us well and held us to the high expectations he had for his students while preparing us for that far away June date. I scored 71%.

I don't remember my English teacher that year. Probably because a significant amount of the curriculum was centered around the reading of two of Shakespeare's works. One was, *you guessed it,* Julius Caesar. I muddled my way through that, again. Disinterested at best and continually annoyed with trying to read the author's written word. Too many *'thees, therefores,* and other sentences and phrases that made no sense to me. And when Caesar Augustus was introduced, I couldn't find my way out of a paper bag if needed. I did, however, know what "et tu Brute" meant. I scored 73% on the English regents in senior year.

Around the same time that I began high school, I was still singing soprano in the choir when my voice literally changed in the middle of the week. Tuesday, I was in the soprano section, and on Friday I found myself with the men in the baritone, bass, and tenor section with other grown men. Now, I only had to attend one rehearsal each week on Friday evening. This opened a door and time in my schedule for me to try out for the basketball team. I did. I didn't make it. Even though I made my first two practice shots while the coaches looked on and I had mentioned that I knew last year's team captain; Ronald, the same Ronald whose footsteps I seemed to be looking to follow. Besides, last year's team had won a championship in the league, and I was a skinny and undersized, young fourteen-year-old.

Years later, I'd hear someone express that, "out of something very bad, comes something very good." Not making the basketball team in tenth grade did not extinguish my fire and desire to be on a varsity team and represent the Lions. Just like at 119, I didn't have to try out for the track team, just show up every day and practice. Our coach, Mr. Dausch, was about five-foot-ten, average stature, wore glasses and was a cigarette smoker just like Mrs. Rohm. He would be my track mentor for three years and my sociology teacher during senior year. Once Mr. Dausch got to know me, and saw that I was reliable, he gave me a coveted hall guard assignment when I had a free or study period on my schedule. As a hall guard, if you saw someone in the halls during class time, they had to show you their pass. Going to the front of the lunch line was a bonus for hall guards. Talk about power. Crossing Guard couldn't touch this. Varsity and Junior Varsity athletes did not have to attend PE class. That seemed odd, but I accepted it, along with the grade of 90% on my report card.

Mr. Nancken, my 11th grade English teacher, asked me to be a cafeteria guard. Again, free lunch came with this. My athletic pursuits had resulted in connecting with two teachers who encouraged a sense of belonging to my days in high school. In Mr. Nancken's class, we were all invited to submit one of our essays in a contest that was sponsored by a Jewish Women's Organization in the area. Low and behold, I won. I was seated in the first row of the auditorium with two other students who were finalists, like me. And I will never forget the jaw-dropping looks that were directed my way by the women representing the organization when I stood up following the reading of my name, "Henry Stafford Van Putten Jr." They even got the pronunciation correct. I walked onto the stage to receive a medal and a Webster's Dictionary. Judging by their initial reaction, I don't think that the white women representing the organization envisioned a handsome, young and apparently intelligent Black high school student winning their contest.

I made another teacher connection with my Speech Class teacher, Mr. Christie who, after a semester in his class, encouraged me to fill out my weekly class schedule by taking Honors Speech during my senior year. This was fine with me as I enjoyed, as I do today, speaking to an audience. I learned to prepare a text from which to speak. More importantly, I learned to be careful of the words I chose, and to know their meaning. In my presentation about the USS Pueblo, I misused the word 'fatal' to describe injuries to the entire crew that was not quite accurate.

"Did everyone on the USS Pueblo die?" Mr Christie inquired when I was done.

"No, just one person." I replied.

"Well then," he gently retorted, "your speech indicated multiple fatalities."

There was an elevator in the building that only students with a special pass could use. If you happened to know someone with one of these passes, the request to borrow it became part of the culture among us. And hall guards, like me, were among the biggest *latchers-on* for taking this ride up and down.

We still had to wear ties. This was a strict rule until the middle of my junior year. If you didn't have one, you were directed to go to the Boys Dean's office to rent one for the day or make one out of paper if the tie supply was already taken. Then hope that your teacher didn't mind the paper one. If so, you'd end up with after-school detention.

I made soap in the chemistry lab during 11th grade. Everyone in class shared a sink with another, and we each had our own little station. I cannot tell you what ingredients were mixed and then held over a bunsen burner because I don't remember. I do remember pouring out the liquid at a point when it was beginning to coagulate. BAM! My own little two-inch by two-inch blob hardened into a usable form of soap. It was without the color and fragrance of store-bought soap. In our home, Ivory was the brand of choice. Rather, it had an industrial scent to it. This was also the year that wearing a tie was no longer required of boys.

We had track practice every day after school. During the indoor season practice was on the speed prohibiting banked track, that was built over the school's basketball court. I say that because you could only have a few folks running at a time, and we'd often have to start on different sides of the banked oval. Maybe that was the reason I came up with a quad strain during the first few days of training. Maybe I was just trying to go faster than the track or my body would allow. I had to sit out a few days, but still attended practices.

The indoor season was a series of city-wide meets on Saturdays in the armory on the upper west side of Manhattan. I had to take the Q40 bus, but this time past Sutphin to Parsons Boulevard to catch the subway, the E train, to 50th Street, then go upstairs to wait on the AA to take me uptown to the armory. Whenever I rode on the subway, I always had to ride in the train's first car. From here I could stand at the front window - right next to the Motorman's cubicle - and look out into the tunnel as the train sped along. Sometimes, I'd have my nose pressed up against the window as I looked out leaving a smudge mark that my Mom would have to wipe clean when we got arrived at our station. Yesterday.

Inside the armory, a 220-yard oval was appropriately called 'the boards' because if you had the misfortune of falling during your race, especially the sprint races, pulling splinters out of your body always followed.

Our so-called locker room area in the armory was near a fleet of motorized military equipment. The smell of diesel fuel permeated the air. A guard in uniform was posted there, to be sure we went in the right direction to change. Our changing area always smelled of liniment cream and oil as runners would generously apply this before heading out for their event. You always had take your things with you.

That season, Mr. Dausch entered me in either the 600 or 880-yard run. Later in my college career, these would still be the distances that I most enjoyed competing at. I ran one minute and twenty-four seconds for the 600, and two minutes and twenty-five seconds for the 880. That's a ten second improvement from my time of 2:35 at 119. Not bad for a skinny, undersized fourteen-year-old.

I continued with the track team into the outdoor season. But this time for practice, we'd have to travel a short city bus ride to the quarter mile cinder track at Victory Field located in Forest Park. School was out by 3 PM and practices began by 3:30 PM. Mr. Dausch was always there before us and probably changed the severity of our workouts to reflect our tardiness and send a message. Then, on other days, we'd go to another nearby park where we'd run the park's hills. Down first, dodging boulders and zigzagging to the bottom, before enduring the pain of doing the return uphill run.

The outdoor season also had some dual meets against rival schools in our district, and several city-wide meets that were held at Randall's Island right under the Tri-Borough Bridge. I took the bus and subway just as if it were a school day for the trek from Queens into upper Manhattan. Once on street level, it was a twenty-minute walk along 125th Street to the pedestrian walk on the Triborough Bridge. After going down a series of staircases, the stadium appeared with its seats surrounding the quarter mile oval. You could see the infamous Rikers Island Jail, just across the river.

The first meet I went to was the Brandeis Relays. I was running on the 'novice' distance medley relay team with the first leg being 880, second leg 440, third leg was 1320 or three-quarters of a mile, and the anchor was one mile. The label 'novice' meant that you had not yet earned a medal in any running event. Breaking your novice, which meant that you had not yet won a medal, was a big deal. My novice status and that of my three teammates was about to change. I ran the second leg and had no idea what I was doing except running fast to keep up. It took me 59 seconds to circle the oval when I handed off the baton to the next runner. Our team finished in second place, and that meant that the four of us 'broke-our-novice' that day. From this point on, I'd be competing in only 'open' races against better competition.

For the dual meets, Mr. Dausch had me running the 880 and I got my time down to 2:12, then 2:07, where I plateaued with those times for not only the remainder of my sophomore season, but most of my junior year as well. I was still only fifteen and had a lot to learn about competing and being the first person across the finish line. During junior year, our team had another 880 runner, whose time was under 2:05. I only remember him as "Rooney" and he often reminded me that his times were faster than mine, and I still couldn't beat him. In hindsight, this proved to be a motivation for me at practices, even though I wasn't bringing my time down in one of my two favorite events.

With Mr. Dausch's guidance and urging, I began doing some serious interval training. Each day varied in speed, power, and the amount of rest between intervals. For example:

- Repetition 330s and 660s at near race speed.
- Up the ladder workouts. This meant that each interval was longer than the previous one. For example, one workout was 220, then 330, followed by a 440 and finishing up with a 660.
- Down the ladder workouts, which began with the longest distance first.
- Down the ladder and up the ladder workouts - 660, 440, 440, 660.
- Up the ladder and down the ladder workouts - 440, 660, 660, 440.

Mix in a day of hills, and I could feel my body breaking down, but also beginning to build back up and recovering quicker in these workouts that were preparing me for the city-wide competition that I would be facing.

Senior year of high school, I decided to do something that I had never done before. Join and run on the Cross-Country Team. In fact, I had a dislike for running cross-country. I was just short of hating it more than anything. But I came to realize that if I wanted to be first across the finish line, running cross-country was the path to take. For the most part, training included a lot of hill work, some interval work, but very little road work. The city-wide meets were held at Van Cortlandt Park in the Bronx. This was a *long* ride on the subway to get to. Starting with my usual route to catch the E train, but then making multiple changes to reach the IRT that would take me to the site in northern Bronx.

Established in 1888, Van Cortlandt Park is over eleven hundred acres. It is the city's third largest and named after the Van Cortlandt family who were prominent in the area during the Dutch and English colonial periods. My dad would sometimes take me there on Sunday afternoons, so that he could watch the cricket matches. Other than innings, batting, bowling (pitching) and fielding, to this day, I don't know much else about the game.

The cross-country races started on the same side of the field where I had watched the cricket matches. There seemed to be hundreds of runners at the start, all lined up, side by side and at the ready to sprint across a field (about a quarter mile) to a narrow trail that would be the course for runners to follow through the forest, up inclines, and down rocky hills until finally reappearing onto a flat run to the finish.

The elite runners were off like a flash and arrived at the trail with hardly any traffic. However, it was a bottle neck on the highway at rush hour for the rest of us in the pack as we neared the narrow trail. I must have crossed the finish line somewhere between 75th and 100th. I endured those workouts and a few of these events at Van Cortlandt to get ready for my senior year. I was just sixteen.

Remember when I wrote about mail time at Camp Brooklyn? And how would my mom send me at least one letter each week in her beautifully meticulous Palmer Method handwriting? During that last summer at camp in 1969, her handwriting changed. Suddenly, it was scraggly and hardly legible. At the time, I didn't think much about it other than her handwriting was harder to read.

One morning in December of my senior year, I was called to the office, and dismissed to go home. When I got there, my dad told me that my mom had a stroke. I rode with her in the ambulance to LaGuardia Hospital. She died two days later. Her funeral was on Christmas Eve, and I carried the cross for the procession into and out of Grace Church and sang with the choir that night at midnight mass.

The Richmond Hill indoor and outdoor track and field records were displayed outside of the athletic office, right next to the bulletin board where Mr. Dausch would post the workouts for the afternoon. As the indoor season began, I had my eyes on the record for the 600-yard run. It was 1:19.4.

The first indoor meet at the armory in January I ran the 600, my time was 1:21.3. I knew I could get that record and then some. The next race I just missed at 1:19.6. And the following race, I ran 1:16.2 for a new school record. I watched proudly as my name was added to the display outside of the athletic office.

Mr. Dausch wanted me to step up in distance and run the 880 at the City Championships. My times from the previous year did not get me into the 'seeded' section with the elite runners. My 600 time, though, had gotten me into the second heat. When the gun sounded, I went right to the front. I heard Mr. Dausch call out "59" as I finished the second of the four laps. As I headed down the boards toward the 660 mark, I heard a voice saying, "you can do this." It was my mom's voice. And as I raced around the last turn, I saw her face right in front of me urging me on, "you can do this," with that beautiful smile; she'd often it direct my way.

I crossed the finish line in 2:01.3!

Mr. Dausch ran over to embrace me and tell me that my time had put me in third place overall. A few moments later, he went to pick up my bronze medal for my best ever effort to date, that had placed me third in the entire City of New York, for my event that indoor season. My time was also a school record. Wow!

There was a blizzard in February of 1969. Schools were closed for several days. I was at home by myself. My dad, who now was working for the Post Office at Kennedy Airport, called to check on me. He also wanted me to call back, ask for his supervisor and tell that person that, there was a gas leak in our home and my dad needed to come home right away. *My dad was asking me to lie.* This caught me off guard, and I initially balked at doing what he requested. Then, in my discomfort, I remembered something he had always told me, "Everything I tell you is for your own good." I made the call, and he made his way home amid the storm.

As the last semester of my senior year began, I was, again, called from class. This time to see my Guidance Counselor, Mrs. Smith. After a greeting and some small talk, she informed me that my records showed I needed three more science credits. Mind you, this is my last semester in high school, and no one caught this until now? Senioritis had already set in for me, as it had for most of the senior class. *And now I have to take an additional class in this final push?* I inquired about my options. Mrs. Smith proceeded to offer me either 'Introduction to Physics' or 'Introduction to Earth Science.' I took the latter. Went to every class. Didn't take any notes. Got a sixty-five on the regents to pass. It was one of the few times that I approached my academics with the "*I got over*" attitude. I did just enough to pass.

The outdoor season couldn't have started any sooner. Again, I had my eye on one of the school records, this time it was the 880 mark of 1:58.0. I had never gone under two minutes for 'the half' but if I wanted that record, that'd be something I'd have to accomplish.

Workouts intensified. There were more repetition 660s that always included a minimum of a 59 second first 440. And then there were the 220s. I had to run a 220 in under 29 seconds, immediately walk across the football field to the start and repeat. Those repetition 220s were pure hell because the rest time between each was being closely monitored by Mr. Dausch, and if I started dragging it, he'd call me to, "Pick it up Van Putten." At the height of my training that season, I'd sometimes do ten to twelve non-stop 220s and that would be my workout.

We had a dual meet against John Adams, a district rival. Their team included a talented 880 runner, Jesse, who had already posted faster times than me. I wasn't feeling quite well that day, and although I ran a 2:03, he easily outraced me to the finish line. I had to get better.

I increased my repetition 440s to under 59 seconds and my repetition 660s to under 1:28.

I started doing 15 to 20, 220s, each under 29 seconds and still with the walk across the football field.

Mr. Dausch named me Team Captain and I proudly displayed this honor on my Richmond Hill jacket.

Captain of the Crossing Guards was a distant memory.

Our next opponent at Woodrow Wilson High School wouldn't offer me the same challenge that I faced against Jesse. So, I knew that I'd have to do the work on my own, just like I had been doing in practice. When I went past the first quarter mile, I heard Mr. Dausch shout out "58." This was just like practice. And when he rapidly moved to midfield as I passed the 660 mark, he shouted out "1:29!" As I dug down deep for the final sprint to the finish, I heard that voice and saw the image of my mom smiling and saying, *you can do this.*

I finished in 2:00.5, a new PR, but still not under that two-minute barrier.

The Borough of Queens Championships were next. I'd have a rematch with my rival Jesse from John Adams on a weekday afternoon, at Randall's Island oval in Manhattan. This time, though, I was chasing a runner from Thomas Edison High School, his name was Ed. I stayed right on his shoulder through a 57s first quarter mile, and Jesse was nowhere to be seen. I kept pressing on after Ed, but just couldn't get past him over the final lap and he finished in 1:57.4. I crossed the line in 1:58.1, just one tenth of a second from the school record. I finally broke the two-minute barrier and finished second, earning a silver medal in the Queens Borough Championships.

I was in a seeded heat for the city's outdoor championship at Randall's Island the following weekend, but I did not run well. There was a quick 55 second first 440 that I wasn't ready for and I finished well behind the leaders in 2:05.

The next week, I was called again to see Mrs. Smith. As I walked down the hallway to her office, all I could think of was that something had happened, and I would not be able to 'walk' with my classmates. Much to my surprise, Mrs. Smith had two really nice things to share with me. First, I had been selected as the Outstanding Student Athlete by the Long Island Press. This was a local newspaper founded in the nineteenth century, and had been serving Jamaica Queens for many years. The second bit of news from Mrs. Smith was that I had been selected to lead the procession of seniors at graduation into the auditorium of the Alden Theatre on Jamaica Avenue carrying the American flag. I was an interesting choice for the role, but the pride I saw on my dad's face as I entered with the flag was indescribable.

My dad, as I previously shared, had served in WWII as a Master Sergeant and company interpreter as part of the invasion force into France the day after D-Day. Over time, I'd not had the best of relationships with him, due mostly to my smart ass thinking that I knew more than he did, and not being as respectful as I should have been. Our eyes met when I took my place on the stage with the other award recipients, and he gave me the look of a proud dad. Now, having children of my own, I know how to send that look. The Long Island Press Award was the only gold medal that I received during my track and field days in high school, and as a Division I athlete in the same sport in college.

MELVIN HALL, STETSON EAST AND BID-WHIST

hen the graduation ceremony ended, and I led my classmates out of the theater carrying the American flag, I found my dad among the masses that had exited the Alden Theater out into the hustle and bustle of Jamaica Avenue. Still dressed in my cap and gown, my dad gave me a big hug, then said, "Follow me," as we turned down 168th Street. Halfway down the block of businesses was a photographer's studio where my dad had arranged for me to have my picture taken to memorialize the occasion of my high school graduation.

I had spoken with the adult leaders at Camp Brooklyn about the requirements to get a job in the 'Y.' They told me the organization was looking for Physical Education Majors, and that the starting salary was about $8500. I enjoyed sports and after my time as a C.I.T. I began to believe that I also enjoyed working with children. So, let's combine the two.

Everyone during their senior year in high school is asked to write a brief something about themselves for the yearbook. Written under my picture in The Archway (our yearbook) is "Physical Education Teacher." To reach this goal, I began looking for colleges that offered a program for this major—physical education—that I had in mind.

I applied and was accepted to Ball State in Indiana, Springfield College in western Massachusetts, and a few others. But when I was accepted and offered the most financial aid from Northeastern University in Boston, I signed, *better still, my dad signed*, on the dotted line, completing all of the FAFSA questions and filling everything in.

The Hub. The Bean. Beantown and surrounding areas would become my permanent residence for the next three and a half decades.

I had two large suitcases, and one smaller one that was tied with a belt to the other, as I made my way to the ticket counter at Grand Central Station in Manhattan. The sun was already beaming through the many ornate windows of the station's main terminal and ticket area. I purchased a one-way ticket to Boston's South Station, and found my way to the correct platform, lugging my three suitcases along with me. The platform was partially filled with commuters heading off to work or other destinations, but I didn't see anyone toting their suitcases along with them, as I was. The train arrived. I found my way to a window seat and plopped my belongings in the adjoining seats, hoping that no one would sit there. As the train departed, it snaked along the underground tunnel for about five minutes before emerging onto the overhead tracks of Park Avenue and into the sunlight of the mid-September morning.

The four-hour train ride up the I-95 corridor passed through Connecticut, Rhode Island, and into Massachusetts. When I arrived at South Station and stepped off the train, suitcases in tow, the first thing I noticed was that not only was the temperature a bit chillier than expected, but the air quality was much cleaner than that of Manhattan. I found a taxi stand and told the driver I was going to, "Northeastern University, Melvin Hall, 90 The Fenway." About fifteen to twenty minutes later, the cab arrived at the destination. I could see that there was a steady stream of male students walking into Melvin Hall. I approached the check-in desk where three upper-class students were waiting to greet me and direct me to my room. When I told them my name, Henry Van Putten, one of them looked on their list where my full name appeared and remarked, "So *you're* Henry Stafford Van Putten Jr? We were expecting a limo and chauffeur to be dropping you off." My mind went back to that morning in the Richmond Hill auditorium when I won the writing contest and the astonishment of the women presenting me with the award. Such is one of the many stories about my name and the assumptions that accompany it. After receiving my ID card, room key, meal card, and mealtimes, I piled myself and belongings into the elevator.

Melvin Hall was located on The Fens, about two blocks from the city's Art Museum in one direction, and less than half a mile to Fenway Park, home of the Red Sox in the other. The Back Bay Fens was a beautifully kept open green space with basketball courts, a soccer field, and several walking trails. It surrounds some of the leading educational, cultural, and medical institutions in Boston, and is an eclectic mix of formal and community gardens.

My roommate, Steve, was a short, black haired, twenty-two-year-old white student from Canada, a freshman too. We had different majors, and other than sleeping in the same room, did not spend much time together outside of Melvin Hall. But, because he had an ID (his driver's license) that showed he was of age, he'd let me borrow it when I wanted to buy some *alcohol*, even though I was underage. I was also six feet tall, not the five-foot seven that was on the ID. So, on the occasions of using his ID, I'd always bend over to look at the items below the counter as the cashier looked at the ID. I also wasn't white, as the picture indicated, but the person behind the counter seemed to be only interested in the 'date-of-birth' before handing it back to me while I was still nervously perusing the items below the counter.

When it was time to eat, my roommate and I left Melvin and turned right to head down an alleyway of about fifty yards that brought us to Hemenway Street. Taking a right turn, it was less than half a block to get to the dining area inside of one of the women's dorms, Stetson East. I could smell the food as we entered and headed downstairs to the crowded dining room. There were all kinds of folks there. For the most part freshmen like myself, but there were a few upper-class folks there to assist. After getting my food and finding a seat with Steve, I noticed a group of Black students greeting, embracing and talking with each other as if they'd known one another. These folks, I'd soon find out, were also frosh. They seemed to have found a belonging that I was still seeking in this new environment.

The next couple of days were Orientation meetings, and at the end of the last, I went to my first college mixer. I knew nobody, just like that first day at The Hill, and decided to head back to the dorm. Along the way, the hunger alarm went off again, and I found The Yellow Submarine, a sub shop in the basement of a building at the end of the alleyway on my route back to Melvin. There was another student being served. Larry (from New Jersey) was black like me, and we soon found out that we both were in Melvin Hall. The next day, as I waited for Larry in the lobby of Melvin to head over for a meal, I met Ronnie (from Boston), Paul (from upstate New York), and Alkie (from Hartford), all black and frosh like me, and we all made our way to Stetson East. Alkie told us he had gotten his name from friends in high school because he couldn't '*hold his alcohol*' and would quickly become inebriated whenever he drank.

The five of us began to look for each other and spend our down time together throughout that first year. None of us shared the same major, but that didn't seem to bother any of us. I had found a way to belong with the four of them.

To get to class each day, I had to walk through the lobby of the women's dorm, Stetson East. Oftentimes, there was a bid whist game with four black students going on. Sometimes there'd be others who had "next" sitting nearby. Truth be told, I wasn't the only one who either was late or missed a class entirely because of the perpetual game of whist. Some days, I'd intentionally bypass Stetson to avoid the seemingly never-ending whist game, to get to class on time, and walk down Forsyth Street to get to a building called Boston Bouvé where the physical education majors had class. I was the only black student in my section of physical education majors, and it felt just like being back in SP class at 119.

Northeastern University is a five-year cooperative education experience. It allowed me to see if, indeed, the field of study I had chosen was right for me. After the first year, students go to school for a semester (three months), then work for the next semester. Over the course of my five years, there was an occasion of doing two semesters of school, followed by two semesters of working.

My co-op advisor, Dr. John Dromgoole, really took care of me. His charge was to help find jobs for me during co-op time. He was flexible enough that I was able to find my own co-op job, and he gave his approval. The job I found was back in Jamaica at Lincoln Park, as a lifeguard in the New York City Mini-Pool Program. The swimming program was for children twelve and under and I could walk to work each morning, return home for lunch, and then return to the pool (three feet deep, twenty yards by ten yards) for the afternoon. I was the Lieutenant Lifeguard in charge and had another young man assigned to the site as well. Making $4.25 an hour for the forty-hour week and banking almost all of it, was a perk that, again, far outdistanced being a Crossing Guard. One day, a group of older teenage kids entered the pool area and did not respond to our requests for them to leave. We decided to close the pool to the younger children. They certainly didn't like this, and neither did we but it wasn't closed for long. A few of the youngsters went home, and when they returned, each had a parent with them. Soon thereafter, the older kids left the pool and did not bother to come back for the rest of the summer. Community support for the young children had won out with no violence, other than some back-talking.

Over time, only one of my co-op assignments did not work out well for me. It was at an organization like the YMCA. My supervisor was a white man with a third-degree black belt. About a month into the job, I found out that he was keeping a diary of my every move (I discovered it in his desk drawer) and writing about my actions, in the most discriminatory language and fashion. When this came to light for me, I immediately contacted my co-op supervisor who got me out of that assignment and into another by the following week, at the League School of Boston. Situated at the time atop a hill in Newton, the school served students with special needs. There were fewer than fifty children in the entire schoolhouse. During my senior year, Dr. Dromgoole arranged for me to return to the League School for my final, three-month co-op assignment, and then remain to complete my Student Teaching requirement in my final semester.

The Yellow Submarine wasn't the only place to grab a bite to eat between and after scheduled mealtimes. "Let's go for some "swimp-fried-rice," was Ron's favorite saying. The Far East Restaurant was less than a mile walk from Melvin Hall on Massachusetts Avenue. I'd say that along with Larry, Paul, and Alkie, we frequented that spot a few times a month.

Another eatery we'd go to was Ugi's Steak and Cheese. Just off the corner of Mass. Ave and Huntington Ave, for less than two dollars, you could get a huge steak and cheese sub with onions and peppers. Occasionally, I'd splurge and have an Italian sausage added to mine, and it was still less than two bucks.

We'd venture to Dudley Station in Roxbury to find yet another fav. Freddie Parker's Fried Chicken. Talk about 'grease city,' several pieces of the famous fried chicken along with an order of either onion rings (my choice) or French fries, created a cholesterol delight for the brave of heart.

Roxbury, Mattapan, and Dorchester were then, and are still today, where a large segment of the black population in Boston can be found. Boston is a relatively small geographic space compared to the size of my hometown. Although one could take the bus from campus to Dudley, I often took the fifteen-minute walk past the Amtrak tracks, and through the projects to get there. Along the way, day or night, there would always be folks outside on their porches or apartment patios, watching you watching them as you walked by. A friendly, "What's up?" Or head nod between folks was the universal greeting to acknowledge affinity.

One night during that first year, a group of us went to a party just off Blue Hill Avenue, near Franklin Park. Similar in size to Van Cortlandt Park in the Bronx, I'd later get to know the park's area as part of my training on the track team.

What I remember most at that party is being introduced to Bacardi 151. I don't know how I got back to the dorm, but I had my first love-making-with-a-toilet encounter early that morning, when I eventually found my way back to my room.

I didn't have a co-op job my first year, but as part of my financial aid package had been awarded 'work-study' monies (15-20 hours per week) to find a job in the community. And I found one at the Roxbury YMCA. Couldn't get away from what was familiar to me. The 'Y' was less than a mile up Warren Street as you came out of Dudley Station. For perhaps the first time in a long time, I was around folks who looked like me. I'd end classes by three in the afternoon and be at the Roxbury 'Y' by 4:30 to begin my shift, it lasted until around 8:30, Monday to Friday. I was basically a 'towel guy' at the front desk, getting to know folks in the community who frequented the facility to play basketball, attend meetings, and use the services offered to benefit themselves and others.

Freshman year, I ran part of both the indoor season (an ankle sprain delayed my start) and outdoor season for the Division 1 Northeastern University Track and Field Team. During the indoor season, we'd regularly compete against Harvard, Braindeis, Tufts, Boston College, and Boston University in dual meets and in the Greater Boston Championship. Then there were the nationwide events (on a similar scale to the Millrose Games) held on the banked boards in the old Boston Garden at North Station. Running a leg of the 4 x 440 for the first time, I was surprised with my speed—51.9 was world shattering for me, although far off of the sub 45s world record at the time. I primarily ran the 880 outdoors, with my times plateauing at 2:02 for the half mile. I knew there was more in the tank for me, and I had to find a way to bring it out. That outdoor season was the first time I included running on the roads as a part of my training. After greeting us at the beginning of practices, Coach Baker would simply say one of two things, Science Museum or Jamaica Pond. Both were five mile runs over some busy streets, through parks, and neighborhoods with the former choice being along the Charles River. Other times, he'd have us run the four miles to a track on the campus of Boston College, meet us there where he'd put us through a short speed workout, before running back to our campus.

Frosh year ended abruptly when all classes were canceled for the rest of the semester in the Spring of 1970, after what has come to be known as the "Kent State Massacre," at Kent State University in Ohio. While attending a peace rally in opposition to the Vietnam War, the Ohio National Guard viciously and maliciously opened fire on the student demonstrators, killing five students and wounding nine others. The impact of the opposition to the war, and being drafted into military service, was felt nationwide, including the Boston area, home to multiple colleges and universities. At Northeastern, anti-war demonstrations boiled over, too, resulting in the city's Tactical Police being called out and marching down the streets of our campus to clear them of anyone. I watched from a rooftop as a few brave souls decided not to move inside. They were clubbed and thrown into the open doors of a police van.

A few weeks following my high school graduation, my dad took me to the local Selective Service Office to register for the 'draft' into military service. However, because I was enrolled in college, my draft status was 2S. I also think my status had something to do with being an only child, but I'm not sure. Those deemed fit for service were listed as 1A. I also remember the 4F status which was given for medical reasons.

I remember a '*draft* lottery *by birthday*' being imposed nationwide at some point during my college years. One year, my birthday, April

20 (4/20) was #39. There was a high likelihood that I would be drafted and deployed to Southeast Asia. My 2S status, however, prevented me from being drafted into military service that year and for my entire time at Northeastern. It's a mixed blessing that I often reflect on.

My first co-op job, courtesy of Dr. Dromgoole, came in the second semester of my second year. I was living in an apartment on Hemenway Street, with a brother named Calvert who was from Washington, DC. He had a different major than me, but we'd always find time to eat out and especially attend parties on our campus, on a nearby campus, or in the community, happening on the weekend or not. Of course, waiting for "next" in the Stetson East Lobby whist game was like an unofficial affinity group time for us. Playing bid whist was just like the "black tree" in the quad of the main campus. This was a communal gathering point for Black students on campus to meet, greet, hang out and pass on information.

Wentworth Institute of Technology, a four-year engineering college, was about a fifteen-minute walk from where I was living. The job, basically a towel guy, gave me a lot of time to learn a game and get to play it well. Badminton. The gentleman who ran the athletic department, my senior by 25 to 30 years, was regularly available to 'play a set' of three games during the down time in the gymnasium area. Initially, Stu would make me run, and run and run, side to side, back and forth, up and down, and every which way but loose in our matches. But over time, I learned how to cover the court with my reach and unleash my own style to counter my opponent's game. Then I figured out how to make an unreturnable serve. It was like being back on the handball courts of Lincoln Park back in Jamaica, Queens, many yesterdays ago. *Oh, yeah!*

I'd head to the Bursar's Office each Friday to collect my check for the week's work. I opened an account at a local bank and saved fifty bucks weekly each time I cashed my little over $100 check.

I began preparing for the indoor season of sophomore year in the fall, with a lot of road work. I wasn't part of the cross-country team that competed, but along with other guys who were also sprinters and middle-distance runners, we ran at the back of the pack having our own individual competitions. Once the season began, I was running either the 600 or, a new event for me, the 1000-yard run. It amounted to an 880 plus one hundred twenty yards. On occasion, I'd also double in a meet on either the mile or two-mile relay teams.

We trained seven days a week and sometimes the double of a morning and afternoon workout. I learned the hard way, that one should not eat before a workout. Tuesdays and Thursdays were midday workouts; around 2 PM at The Cage on Huntington Avenue where we trained on a 160 yard, four corner, banked track. And there I was, early in the season, having a hamburger and fries around 12:30 PM when a teammate told me that practice was at 2 PM. *Yes, I brought up my lunch during practice.* More importantly, I had a conversation with Coach Baker about my diet. His suggestion of having my favorite hot cereal each morning would allow for the quickest absorption digestively. Ironically, the body's systems were part of the Anatomy and Physiology curriculum that semester. I still eat hot cereal a few times each month.

We had indoor practice most Sunday mornings at The Cage. Early in the season, on Saturday night, I went with a group of friends to a private party just off Beacon Street at an apartment that was part of Boston University. It was about a twenty-minute walk from my room on Hemenway Street.

When the door opened and I walked inside, the room was encircled in a cloud of marijuana smoke. I had never, up to that point, smelled that 'weed' smell. I didn't cough, just breathed normally and inhaled. We didn't stay long as the place, although jumping, was packed with folks.

The next morning at practice, my head and the track were both a constant circle, and running was not going to happen. I feigned illness to be excused.

The 1971 Indoor New England Championships were held on the Campus of the University of Connecticut in Storrs. I always saw the sign on the interstate, when I would take the four-hour ride on the Greyhound Bus from Boston to the Port Authority in Manhattan, indicating the exit for UCONN.

I'd be running the lead off leg of our two-mile relay. The 220-yard indoor oval at UConn was the same distance familiar to me from my high school days, running at the Armory. That was a plus. As the gun sounded to start the race, another runner dashed to the front, just like in my last high school race. This time, though, I was ready for that early move. I got right on his shoulder, straddling the first two lanes.

I heard Coach Baker call out, "58," halfway through my run.

No one got past me, and I didn't pass the leader either. But I had done my job and handed off the baton, a step behind to our next runner in second place, after a 1:58.1 lead off; my best ever indoor half mile. The rest of our team ran much faster than I had but would stay in that same position, second place, through the finish line in 7:45.3. The second-place finish had earned the four of us *All-New-England Honors* in the two-mile relay at the meet. That was a big deal for me!

The season for fall of 1972 came in the wake of the recent Olympics in Munich, Germany. The athletic successes for many throughout those summer games was overshadowed by a terrorist attack that took the lives of several Israeli athletes, in the Olympic Village. One athlete in particular, though, had drawn my attention on the track. Dave Wottle's finish in the 800-meter run final became a personal rallying point in my track career. Wottle, wearing his identifying baseball cap in the competition, earned the gold medal by coming from last to first in the final 400 meters, passing Evgeni Arzhanov of Ukraine (then part of the Soviet Union), in the last stride of the race. It reminded me of that day at Camp Brooklyn when my last stride had won a race, against Fred.

I developed hip tendonitis that season due to the increased amount of road work I was doing. The inflammation took a long time to heal and, as a result, I ended up sitting out the entire indoor and outdoor season.

Finally, as the weather warmed in early June, I was ready and able to continue my training. It was also time to return home for the summer. This meant that I would be doing a lot of running on my own. I knew that as soon as I returned to Boston in the fall, the coaches would know if I had been keeping up my training.

Northeastern owned a camping area in Ashland, MA. For a week in early September, the cross-country team was there doing double workouts each day. Along with a couple of sprinters and a few middle-distance runners like myself, we also spent the week training twice a day with the intention of participating in the cross-country races in the fall.

I never liked running cross-country, but the path to my success would end up by me doing exactly that. One of the runners was my training partner, Paul. Coming out of high school in MA, Paul was a nationally ranked and highly recruited quarter miler. He'd become my new target, just as Fred, Jesse, and Ed had been in my running career. He and I would finish within 5 seconds of each other in the cross-country meets that we competed in that fall.

We had an indoor meet at Dartmouth College in Hanover, New Hampshire. When we were lining up for the 600, I noticed that there were two very large runners (they would turn out to be shot putters) lining up in the lanes on either side of me. When the gun went off, they took off just as fast as me, and as we went around the first bank in the stagger, I suddenly had my legs taken out from under me, as someone was actually doing a rolling block beneath me. I tumbled head-over-heels as the remaining two runners, Paul being one, continued on. Fortunately, I wasn't seriously hurt, and Paul would tell me later, "Sorry about that Hank. When those guys asked me who Paul was, I pointed to you. I don't know why, but I've had others try to take me out in the same way in a race." As displeased as our coach was, he was quite disappointed in the tactics of the opposing coach. I don't recall us returning to that campus again for a competition. After that, I made it a point to always get out fast and be the first to the break where I could control my race and avoid this kind of embarrassment.

Next on the schedule was a tri-meet with two schools in Maine. When we arrived after a two-hour bus ride, a snowstorm was in its early stages. I ran the 600 that day, finishing third in just under 1:16. The snowstorm, raging during the meet, had subsided but delayed our departure for several hours. Several of the *female* spectators were also stuck at the fieldhouse. Somehow, my teammate Walter (whom I'd room with the following year) approached Coach Cohen with their dilemma. Incredibly, the coach gave Walter the keys to his car, to drive them a short distance to their apartment on the other side of campus.

"Wanna come along, Hank?" He quietly said so no one would hear.

"Why not?" I responded with a bit of deviousness in my voice.

Those young ladies cooked a meal for the two of us and wanted us to stay longer than the hour or so that we were there.

"What took you so long?" Coach Cohen asked Walter when we returned. "And why is Hank with you?"

Always the quick thinker, Walter responded without missing a beat, "There was a lot of snow to move off your car and dig it out. Hank helped."

"Get on the bus!" I could hear his knowledge of calling *bs* to Walter's response in his voice.

The Greater Boston Championships were two weeks away. Coach told me I'd be running the 600 and two-mile relay. The 600 had three trial heats, and the fastest five times would compete in the final the following day. I remembered my experience from Dartmouth and was determined to get to the break first, where I could manage my position in lane four. I did and finished the heat in 1:12.4. Unfortunately, my fast time didn't make the finals, but I had a new PR.

Running only the two-mile relay the next afternoon, I slept past 9 AM, had my hot cereal for breakfast, and headed over to the Cage for the short bus ride to Harvard's indoor bubble. Disappointed, yet ready, I got the stick in fourth place and took off after the runners ahead of me. When I passed Coach Baker, I heard him call out. "53, 54," for my first 400. I'd never gone that fast before and wasn't about to stop then. I'd catch two of the runners ahead of me, and my teammates held that position for a second-place finish.

"Hank, wanna know your time?" Coach Cohen approached me with a big grin on his face, "1:53.8." For me, a new PR in the 800, albeit on a relay leg. Still, Wow!

The following week were the New England Championships at the Coast Guard Academy in New London, Ct. We arrived in the evening after the almost two-hour bus ride from Boston. Walter, who was a long and triple jumper and has turned out to be a lifelong friend, and I shared a room.

The next morning, I had to run in one of four, 600 trial heats with the top eight running in two sections for the Finals. My time of 1:13.7 in the second heat had me waiting with nervous anticipation to see if I had made the Finals. Seeming like the longest time to run those next two heats and waiting to hear, Coach Cohen again approached me to say that my time was one tenth of a second better, and I had made the Finals. I would be in the first of the two heats for the Finals.

With my dad, who had made the trip from Jamaica that day, cheering me on, I was the first across the finish line in my heat; 1:11.6 was not only a PR, but only six-tenths of a second from the school's record. The four runners in the second heat would beat my time by less than half a second, and I would end up finishing fifth overall. *Wow!* All the training was paying off in a big way for me. *Yesterday.*

THE PHONE IS RINGING

The Northeastern University graduating Class of 1974 assembled at the old Boston Garden on Sunday, June 16, 1974. The thousands of graduates, all adorned in our caps and gowns, were waiting in the same area that the Ringling Brothers Circus used for its animals. If I could attach a smell to Noah's Ark, this would be it.

As we waited to process into the vast arena where family and friends awaited us, my thoughts turned to my dad. Just as my mom had not lived to see me graduate from high school, my dad had been taken by cancer in March of that year. I had gone home to see him for the last time about a month before he became an ancestor. He would not be there to see the event he had worked so hard for me to achieve. His youngest brother, my Uncle Earl, his wife Julia, and a childhood friend, Jacques, from my choir days whom I had adopted as my little sister, made the four-hour car ride from Jamaica, Queens to be there for the big event. My first wife, Joyce, pregnant with my first child, Jamal, sat in the seat next to them. Dad had met Joyce on a few occasions, and never offered an opinion to me about how he felt about my marriage nor his impending first grandchild. I had not always been as respectful to my dad as I grew up and went off to college. It's something that I regret to this day. Walking onto the floor of the Garden that day, I was numb to the feelings of being alone as

I watched the assembled family members of others revel in the joy of the moment for their graduating senior.

Soon after graduation, I was blessed to meet two men, both now ancestors, who would help to lay the path of my professional career—even though I didn't know or appreciate it at the time. Both Sam and Al, black men, were well established principals in their respective suburban communities. They had made an important commitment to themselves to recruit black educators for theirs, as well as other communities that stretched all along the Route 128 corridor.

After an interview with Sam, he guided me in completing several applications for the role I was seeking—Elementary Physical Education Teacher—in multiple suburban districts in the Boston area. All the applications, although unique to their respective districts, had one similarity. In the upper right-hand corner of the first page was a green mark, about one inch in length. Initially, this caught me off guard as to why I kept seeing this signifier on each of the applications I completed. Then it dawned on me. My application was being flagged as being submitted by a person of color. In the wake of the country's struggles with affirmative action, it appeared that these school districts were trying to bring in candidates of color for teaching positions.

In mid-July, I traveled with my wife, Joyce (now several months pregnant) to Sandusky, Ohio to see her mom. It was a non-stop almost twenty-four-hour drive across Massachusetts, then New York State and finally crossing into Ohio, all on Interstate 90. Sandusky was west of Cleveland and as the sun began to rise, the interstate signs telling the distance to our destination began to appear.

We stayed for several days, then headed back taking a different route through Pennsylvania to stop and see a friend of mine from St. Albans, Vel, who was attending Penn State University. The winding hills through the state often had us right on the edge of the highway with only a guard rail between my Spirit of America Chevy Vega, and a perilous fall over the edge.

Throughout the trip, I had a recurring dream that the phone was ringing in our apartment back in Boston on Huntington Avenue on Northeastern's campus. The afternoon we got back, I fortunately found a parking space right near the entrance to our residence on Huntington Avenue. As I opened the door to the apartment, the phone was ringing. It was Newton Public Schools contacting me to offer me a job as an Elementary Physical Education Teacher. Captain of the Crossing Guards was now a distant memory.

When I entered the cafeteria at Newton North High School on the Tuesday after Labor Day, I was reminded of the feelings I had experienced on that first day of tenth-grade at Richmond Hill High School. Except for Sam, an elementary principal himself in Newton, I didn't know anybody among the assembled gathering, that numbered in the hundreds. Names were being called out, and greetings offered between folks to catch up on what each had been doing since the ending of school. I was wearing a jacket (where I attached my name tag) and pants that matched to make them appear as a suit. They were a combination of the colors of desert sand and a blueish gray. A solid blue shirt and tie to match, a full afro neatly combed out and a pair of Florsheim shoes topped off my first day look. Sam saw me, I exhaled, and we headed toward one another. Walking alongside him was an older white man whom I would shortly find out was the principal of the Bowen School, Jack McLeod. We greeted one another and he gave me directions to the school and suggested I come to the office when I arrived. We found a seat as the program began.

The seventy-five minute program included welcome back speeches and words of support for the upcoming year made by the Mayor, The School Committee Chair, and The Head of the NTA (Newton Teachers Association). A special performance by students (elementary, middle and high school) of singing, band and orchestra selections allowed me to see a piece of the culture I was about to enter. I liked music that sounded good, and these selections sounded good! The last to speak was the Superintendent, who would always begin with noted accomplishments and ongoing work being done in the district. They would also often outline the direction of the district, the goals for getting there and end with words of support, before we'd head back to a faculty meeting at our respective schools. First year teachers, like myself, were invited to an afternoon gathering to complete paperwork for orientation. What stands out in my mind from that day was joining the NTA (Newton Teachers Association) and immediately being eligible for health care benefits. Benefits that to this day I remain privileged to have. With the exception of the first-year teachers meeting, I'd be doing most of the same early September routine, including that initial school faculty meeting, for most of the next 35 years.

My assignment and schedule that first year, saw me at two of the district's twenty-three elementary schools; three days at Bowen School, and two at the Hamilton School which had the smallest population of students in the district. Bowen, on Cypress Street in Newton Centre, became a part of my assignment and schedule, and my home school, for the next 18 years. The last several years, it was the only school for my full-time 1.0 assignment. I'm still in touch (in person and by social media) with many of these former students, all grown with children (and grandchildren) of their own. My heart is touched when they share remembrances of our times together playing with the parachute, or doing a gymnastic show, or singing while exercising to the song Chicken Fat. One recently expressed that she is teaching her children the lessons of FOHGYCB ("finding out how good you can be") that I had taught her in PE class. More on what those initials mean is coming.

After orientation, I followed the directions given to me to 280 Cypress Street, site the Bowen School. I found a space in the parking lot for teachers and headed inside to find the office, where I was greeted by the school's Secretary, Evelyn. She was a short of stature, white woman with graying hair and an affectionate smile that peered out over her glasses. She said that Jack had told her to expect me as she handed me a key to my office, an envelope and then glided over to the mailbox area to point mine out.

After the faculty meeting on the second floor in the school's library, I returned to the first floor, and made my way to the gymnasium. Not knowing what to do, I decided to see what equipment I had available. So, I removed my jacket and then, I spent the next hour or so taking inventory. I found quite a bit in that closet; all different sizes of playground balls, basketballs, soccer balls and volleyballs, each in its own netted bag. Parachute. Bean bags. Scooters. Much more than I can remember, but I included it in my count.

That first year of teaching remains a blur to me because in December of that year, my first son, Jamal, was born. Joyce had a difficult pregnancy with multiple false labors in the closing weeks before his birth. Coincidentally, he was born one day short of nine months after my dad had died.

With the help and support of a veteran elementary PE teacher, Marty, I worked hard to earn "tenure" after my third year at Bowen. In addition to the Bowen School, my schedule continued to be filled out at a different school each year. What was ironic, and somewhat troubling, was that the second school to which I was assigned, seemed to close at the end of that year. Hamilton School. Emerson School. Spaulding School. And when the Countryside School was part of my assignment as year four began, it too, was a school under consideration for closing, due to declining enrollment. I couldn't let go of the feeling that the school closings had something to do with me. However, at the end of the academic year, it, too, was spared the chopping block.

HALLELUYAH! My new assignment would now be 1.0 at the Bowen School for the upcoming academic year. No more traveling between two schools. Over time, this would turn out to be sweeter than being a Crossing Guard.

LEARNING TO MOVE AND MOVING TO LEARN

"*L*earning to Move and Moving to Learn." That was the ten-foot-long multi-colored banner I made and taped over the entrance to the gymnasium. And I insisted that my students refer to our work as physical education, *not* gym. It was the Physical Education Center and they learned to respect that name, even up to this very day with those that I am still in contact with. And if someone errors and posts a comment on social media that says, "gym," others will quickly and politely remind them of our time in "Physical Education."

In the late 1970s, I'd met a colleague, also teaching at Bowen, who I would describe as one of my best friends. Kemp, a Black, gay man, was one of the four K-1 teachers. After provisioning my class space each morning, I'd spend the first part of my day sitting in his classroom greeting his five year olds. I always had a cup of tea as we sat near the sandbox, shooting the breeze until 8:50 when I'd make my way back to the PE Center for my first class.

Kemp was then, and is today, loved and respected by colleagues, students, and parents throughout the community. He has defined his retirement by doing what he loves most; creating and performing music based on his life experiences. Many families would request to have their child in his classroom. Some had had another child experience the magic of his teaching style, while others had heard-through-the-grapevine about his work with students.

Kemp, as I stated above, is a talented musician who brought that part of his love of life into the space for his students. He could seamlessly move a student with the side-eye of desisting, while simultaneously holding the attention of others with wit, enlistment, and *plain old love.*

As our friendship grew, we would continue our daily routine for over a decade, and spend some great times going to concerts (Freddie Jackson), jazz clubs (to see Najee), and performances at the Wang Center in Boston by artists such as Savion Glover, Ladysmith Black Mambazo, and the Alvin Ailey American Dance Theater. I've often said to others that if you have a friend like my friend Kemp, you have a blessing beyond words.

When I leased a brand-new Nissan Maxima, I invited Kemp to stop by and check it out. He drove the five-speed manual shift out of our driveway, me in the passenger seat and we headed out for a ride.

"Where to?" Kemp inquired.

"Let's head out to the Mass. Pike. I've got something I want to do."

"Let's go!" Was his response as we headed for Newton Corner and an entrance to The Pike.

On our short five-minute ride to the highway, I opened the car's moonroof.

"Nice!" Was his response.

Once on the highway, I did something I've always wanted to do. Stand up in the passenger's seat, while going over seventy miles per hour. With the wind whipping across my face, I held my balance, then extended my arms out and had my Leo DeCaprio moment as if I were *on-top-of-the-world.* When the exit sign appeared, I brought my arms in and sat my butt back down as we headed back home.

One of my favorite times of the year was teaching gymnastics, which started right after the Christmas break and continued for six weeks right up to the Winter break. But being a favorite didn't start out that way. In fact, I almost lost my job. My mentors—who now also included Dave, Lee, Scott, and Dick—provided me with safety guidelines and sequential steps for teaching floor exercise, balance beam, parallel bars, uneven bars, pommel horse, and vaulting. I was an eager learner, especially when it came to safety, matting of an area, and correct spotting technique for my students. In addition, there were three climbing ropes at one end of the gymnasium. This station was also matted beneath the ropes for climbing only. No swinging on the ropes was allowed. Toward the end of the unit in February, a student did not follow this rule as expected, fell, missed the mat, and injured themself. The child's parents decided to sue the district and called for my termination due to negligence. After what seemed like months of legal wrangling, including more than one deposition in a downtown Boston attorney's office I had to give (represented by the NTA'a counsel), the suit was settled. I kept my job and earned my tenure as a teacher.

I said that teaching gymnastics to K-6 students was one of my favorite times of the school year. And in the many years that followed, it certainly was. But during that year, I also began my journey toward earning a Masters Degree by taking a course in Behavior Modification. Taking this course completely changed my approach to teaching, by learning to incorporate positive reinforcement into my repertoire of teaching. Here's what I mean.

All of my PE classes (K-6) began at the center jump circle of the basketball court. When the students entered, my expectation was for each to be seated around the circle. As you might expect, there were those who found this difficult to do. But rather than calling them on their off-task behavior, I learned to recognize those who were seated to await the beginning of class.

"Jean, thanks for finding the circle."

"Reggie, I appreciate how you are following directions."

"Sarah, great job and example you are setting for your classmates."

"Great job, Michael."

There are hundreds of ways to give positive affirmations to students and each day I'd find a new one.

Two things began to transpire over time. First, I was getting to know the names of students, which is arguably the most important aspect of their identity. Second, those who were having difficulty finding the circle wanted to hear their name called, too, for appropriate behavior like their classmates. And the only way to make that happen was to find a seat at the circle. It became easier to connect with students and changed the atmosphere from compliance to community. I credit Dr. Frank Rife, who taught the course, with opening the door to becoming the best teacher and version of myself possible. Finding off-task behavior is not hard to do. But rewarding on-task behavior would get me exponentially more mileage with my students in the years to come. In those yesterdays, I was learning the value of developing my attention and momentum strategies for the classroom, which I still carry with me today.

Picture this in the Physical Education Center. A fifty-foot-long floor exercise length of mats, matted areas with a low and a high balance beam, parallel bars, uneven bars, pommel horse, and vaulting. Twenty to twenty-four students equally divided and working at each of these stations. Now, snap a finger as *loud* as you can, ten times. While I spotted at the uneven bars, with a proximity to see the entire room, that finger snap was my signal to stop, look, and listen for instructions. It was beautiful to be a part of and see, as the community of students worked and supported each other. For grades K-2, I worked with our 6th grade teachers (Carolyn and Sofia) to create a Gymnastic Helpers group. These students would be taught how to support the younger students in safely using the equipment. Those in grades 3-6 were provided with a sequence of skills (written and neatly placed in a folder taped to the wall) that included routines for each piece of equipment. When reaching a point that required spotting, I was available to provide the needed support. The students respected the equipment.

At the end of the unit, each of the 4th to 6th grade classes (two at each grade) were given the opportunity to put together a Gymnastics Show for the entire school. Although voluntary, almost every student in those six classes was eager to show their skills for everyone on the big day. I picked the music (always a Top 20 song of the day), Kemp would DJ, and it was a glorious time for the performers, those watching in awe and invited guests (parents and administrators from the central office), as our community of learners bonded even more.

Teaching gymnastics and putting together the show was one of my favorite times during the school year. Another was the volleyball unit for grades 4 to 6. The gym was set up with two side-by-side volleyball courts. This time, sitting at the center circle was replaced with students immediately going to their assigned 'warm-up' court. Three at the net. Three on the back line. Those at the net would practice overhead sets and bumping with a partner on the opposite side of the net, while the students in the back right of the court would practice their serve. The other two on the back line retrieved the ball and passed it to whomever was in the service area of the court. That's ten volleyballs all in motion, while students waited for my whistle (which I rarely used indoors) to "rotate clockwise in your court" to the next position. It was the warm-up routine that the students owned. I continued to get great mileage from the positive reinforcement strategies I had learned.

Beginning in the early to mid-1980s, the district had undertaken a multi-year professional development for teachers based on the work of Dr. Jonathan Saphier and Robert Gower, co-authors of 'The Skillful Teacher.' The repertoires of teaching that the authors outline and supported with empirical data, came under big umbrella headings that included management, instructions, motivation, and curriculum. Embracing these strategies was the next step in my professional journey. Instead of looking at learning through the lens I had grown up with, I redefined learning through the banner, also over the entrance to my teaching space. I taught from a belief that *learning is a change in behavior.* Not from the typical compliance or rote way of learning, but rather from changing the behavior in approaching a task. If one behavior is ineffective, move on to another where you can be successful and feel good about yourself. I changed the signage in the PE Center from the traditional list of *DOs, DON'Ts, and NOs* to represent this way of thinking. They were displayed around the space, reviewed at the beginning of each new school year, and reinforced throughout the ensuing ten months during PE class and beyond into the culture of the entire school. They read:

- Avoid blame.
- Avoid bringing low.
- Speak for yourself.
- One person speaks at a time.
- Leave the equipment neater than you found it.
- Everyday F.O.H.G.Y.C.B.

It was the mid to late 1980s when the district undertook another bold step in professional development. The district superintendent, Irwin Blumer, made an announcement at the initial school wide gathering in September that I previously described which garnered everyone's attention in the auditorium.

The words were something to the effect of, "This year, our goal is to raise the academic achievement of Black students to that of white students in this district." The auditorium became silent. The eyes of everyone around me were fixated toward the lectern on the stage, seemingly anxiously awaiting what was to follow. The Superintendent presented district-wide data that identified this "gap in learning" with specifics from discipline referrals, to GPAs, and enrollment in AP and Honors Classes as evidence that the district needed, could and would do better. Four, full day seminars, based on the work of the Efficacy Institute, under the direction of it's founder and President, Dr. Jeffrey Howard provided the focal point.

Dr. Howard's work presented a new paradigm for individual development. It ran in opposition to the traditional linear, one way "American model" of development which operated under the belief that each person is born with a certain package of material.

The American model reflects a belief that students often feel and act in a way that says "Some are smart. Some are kind of smart. Some are dumb." In addition to some teachers, students supported and acted on this belief. His research uncovered the negative impact of this kind of thinking on the academic achievement of students with a practical principle:

Thoughts -> Actions.

The way one thinks of themself in a particular situation will determine the action they take. In this model of development, one's belief in their innate ability (being born smart or not) determined how much one can develop. And when that is believed, it becomes a self-fulfilling prophecy and a fixed mindset. It reads this way:

Ability -> Development.

By contrast, Dr. Howard's Efficacy Model (mobilizing available resources to solve problems and promote development) believes that learning is incremental. This kind of growth mindset is also reflected in the work of renowned Stanford Professor Dr. Carol Dweck.

I would present this new paradigm about development to my students each September when we met for the first time in the PE Center. When compared to the previous model, it reads:

Confidence -> Effort -> Development.

Many students, myself included, benefitted from visual learning as represented by this diagram. It was displayed prominently on one wall.

As confidence builds, one's effort becomes more effective. Development is furthered.

With my students, I would break it down to their age level of learning by tenaciously saying throughout our time together each year "If you think you can (confidence)->And make an **effective** effort (effort)->You will get smart (development). Smart is something that you earn. Not something that you are!"

F.O.H.G.Y.C.B.

F.O.H.G.Y.C.B (Foh-Gi-Ch-Bee - Find Out How Good You Can Be) became my overarching objective for each student in PE. And the culture that these words represent extended throughout the schoolhouse for everyone to embrace.

As part of a running unit in the fall, the 5th and 6th grade students would gather data on their pulse recovery, graph their results in math class, then respond to guided questions for discussion in PE. F.O.H.G.Y.C.B.

Charlotte, our music teacher, invited me to assist her with the school's music production each spring. F.O.H.G.Y.C.B.

2nd and 3rd graders learned how to play floor hockey. White shoe polish designated the areas of the floor for each position. Everyone wore safety goggles and always kept the blade of their plastic hockey stick on the floor. Students waiting their turn sat safely behind a stack of mats for the next rotation that happened every two minutes. F.O.H.G.Y.C.B.

3rd and 4th graders completed a Bicycle Safety Program under the supervision of Officer Cindy Webster of the Newton Police Department. In So Doing, students earned permission to ride their bikes to and from school each day. F.O.H.G.Y.C.B.

Kindergarteners and 1st graders discovered how to move in the space around them and explore the basic concepts of catching (thumbs up or pinkies down) and throwing (opposite foot forward, eye on the target, twist, throw and follow through). F.O.H.G.Y.C.B.

And everybody loved playing together as one team with the parachute to make different overhead shapes, sit inside, cross underneath or going outdoors to launch playground balls into the air and catch. F.O.H.G.Y.C.B.

As much as I enjoyed teaching the eight weeks of gymnastics, or the six weeks of volleyball, or even playing with the parachute, I *really* loved teaching track and field for eight weeks each spring for all our students. This would begin right after our Spring Break in April when the New England weather still hadn't decided if it was time for springtime temperatures, or not. For the K-3 students, I brought out the white shoe polish again, erased a few of the floor hockey lines, to draw a three-lane track around the perimeter of the gymnasium. F.O.H.G.Y.C.B.

Meanwhile the 4th, 5th, and 6th graders were participating in the Spring Olympics. Each class was divided to represent a country on one of four continents; Africa, Asia, North America, Europe, and each country earned points for drawing their country's flag on a pre-measured piece of oak tag I'd distribute. Each team was scoring

points within their class, and that was added to other teams from that continent in other classes.

What followed were three outdoor classes of trying out these events:

- 6-pound Shot Put.
- High Jump using a "scissor kick."
- Long Jump.
- Triple Jump.
- Low Hurdles.
- 50 and 100-meter dash.
- Relay.

It was like being the coach of a team, the way that the students enthusiastically practiced.

As with volleyball, four team captains (representing the diversity of the class) were chosen. Each captain selected teammates, alternating between selecting a girl and a boy and gathered to completed their entry form. Then I led one last practice. If it rained, the gym provided the perfect space to teach and practice the shot put, high jump, sprint starts, and finishes over the length of the PE Center. Two large mats against one wall helped to safely brace their finish. The continent scores were posted in the gymnasium and on Fridays, I'd make my rounds about the schoolhouse to wish everyone, "Have a great weekend!" And share the up-to-date scores in the classes involved. F.O.H.G.Y.C.B.

Each year, the school's PTA would work with me on different events. One was Earth Day, that was a successful precursor of the international expressions we see each year around the theme of re-use, reduce, and recycle. The PE Center was transformed into the greenery found in the greenest of forests. I dressed as a turtle for the day.

A second was to prepare the student population and parents for Color Day. This end-of-the-year day-long annual event, was a non-competitive and fun-filled day for the entire community., We had some fourteen stations, inside and out, and used several of the PE activities the students were familiar with. Two or three parents ran each station's activity. Teachers stayed with their class as they moved from one event to the next. With lunch in the middle of the day, including an ice cream treat from the PTA, and a rest period that followed lunch, it seemed to mirror and reminded me of those special days at Camp Brooklyn, many yesterdays ago. F.O.H.G.Y.C.B.

QUICK FAST AND IN A HURRY. THOU SHALT NOT PASS

I was leaving Kemp's home in Cambridge and heading home to Newton going westbound on Mass, Pike about 6 PM. It was a spring evening in the mid-1980s with the sun setting in the west and glaring right in my direction on the interstate. Right after the Allston tollbooth as I headed out onto the highway, another car pulled in behind me and began flashing their high beams at me. I could see it wasn't a State Trooper's car, and I almost didn't pull over into the breakdown lane, but I did. And out of the car enthusiastically emerged a former runner from Northeastern University, where I too had been a track athlete. Mark Lech's career as a runner had far exceeded mine as he had thrust himself into the national spotlight of elite middle-distance runners during his time as a Northeastern Husky and then with Athletics West, an American running team formed in 1977 by the legendary Bill Bowerman co-founder of Nike, Inc.

I'd not seen Mark in several years but there we were, safely in the breakdown lane on the Mass Pike, greeting one another like old friends. During a few moments of catching up, I mentioned to him that I was teaching elementary physical education and doing a little coaching at Weeks Junior High School. Mark then shared that when he had noticed my vanity license plates (HVP II), he took the opportunity to talk to me about coaching outdoor track and field with him at one of the high schools in the district where I worked.

Well, this would be a dream come true and I jumped at our chance encounter to take on the role of Assistant Coach at Newton North High School. I'd be working with the sprinters, jumpers, and pole vaulters. The latter I knew nothing about. But soon I sought out and found myself attending coaching sessions, coincidentally at the same facility—The Cage—where we had both practiced and competed on the campus of Northeastern.

I also went to coaching skill sessions to learn more about training and technique for our hurdlers, long, high, and triple jumpers. During some practices, Mark, who also triple jumped in high school, would compete with our group in their own jumping events.

One afternoon, they talked trash back-and-forth and he loved it!

"What are you out here trying to do, old man?" One of the jumpers directed it toward Mark, as he stretched to prepare.

"I'm out here to out jump YOU", Mark snapped back, pointing his finger at the one who had called him out. "Let's go!", Mark continued in a boasting and confident tone.

"Don't hurt yourself now," another jumper chimed in.

"I don't see you out here. C'mon!" Mark spread his arms wide apart as if to call them all out.

This kind of friendly teasing was a part of our team culture. There'd be times when we'd need to come down harder in their preparation. And there'd be other times, like this, when it was just fun to be around a group of folks working toward a common goal.

Fortunately for me, the hurdlers had a good foundation before I arrived as their coach, and as I watched them work, I added the learning from the coaching sessions to what I was learning from them. Then I took their work, and added a little something to it from what I was observing in others, in the event as we'd compete against other schools during the season.

I found the sprinters (anything 400 and under) was the group I had to earn the respect of more so than the others. With them, I often shared my nine years running career, although I was a middle distance runner, in the same events. I contacted the coach, my counterpart, at the other high school in the district to get permission to come over to their oval one afternoon. I ran with them the two and a half miles there, had them do a short workout on their track, and ran back together. Just as I had done in my yesterdays at Northeastern.

One afternoon, I introduced them to a tried-and-true training method *fartlek.*. It's a German word that translates to speed play. I included the hurdlers and jumpers in this workout, too. That's about two thirds of the whole team of over forty.

I spread them out in pairs and trios around our quarter mile oval (maybe 10 to 15 meters apart) and then I stood at the top of the stadium steps. They'd begin walking, then full out sprint on the sound of my whistle to try and catch the next group. I called it *'quick-fast-and-in-a-hurry'* which would become a favorite fun saying among the group and the team. I'd change the time between whistles, incrementally going up, then down. This would continue for about 30 minutes. And during this time, I'd make it a point to call out each runner's name for their effort with positive reinforcement. Just like I had learned to do with my students at Bowen. I had a big voice, and it came in handy in leading this workout from the football stands.

Otis Street. Simply hearing me say that name sent a message to them that most dreaded power-workout I'd have them do was on the agenda for the afternoon. Otis Street ran perpendicular to Lowell Avenue and was one block from the school's entrance. While each did their stretching at the bottom, I began the about three-hundred-yard ascent, up the street at about a ten-to-fifteen-degree incline. Their first attempt was always the fastest. A few even topped their time for the second run. But oh, that third time was *painful.* When my former student athletes and I chat online, the topic of Otis Street often comes up.

I was teaching our runners what would eventually become the motto of our sprint group; *thou shalt not pass.* Remember that 10 to 15 meters apart? *Thou shalt not pass.* Over time, I began to shorten the distance to less than 10 meters when they began. *Thou shalt not pass.*

We had a good team that scored among the top teams at both Regional and State meets. Cambridge Ringe and Latin High School was a formidable foe in our league as well. The year we finally outscored them in a dual meet brought a lot of respect from our opponents and a sense of, you know, *FOHGYCB,* for the team members during our celebration in the locker room. For the four years I was there, the Newton North 4 x 400 team was known as one of the best in the state to compete against, both indoors and outdoors. One year, they were recognized by a local newspaper, the Boston Herald, for the newspaper's All-Indoor Team.

GOING OVER TO THE OTHER SIDE

I had been working to complete my Master's Degree over a number of years since taking that Behavior Modification course, almost a decade ago. I learned through the grapevine that when a student teacher, from one of the many universities in and around the Boston area, came to our district to complete their Student Teaching and earn their degree, a voucher for taking a three-credit graduate course at that university accompanied them. I got to know the person who had the responsibility to oversee these vouchers (for Harvard, Wheelock, Boston College, Bridgewater State, and others) and over the years I completed almost all the requirements to earn my degree for free! Free, in the sense that I was able to access and use several of these vouchers, while at the same time supporting a prospective teacher in their journey as a student teacher in the PE Center. By September of 1988, I had the finish line in sight and enrolled in a program at Cambridge College to complete my degree work by December. I loved teaching PE, but I wanted to be a building Principal.

The Cambridge College graduation ceremony was on a sunny and brisk Sunday afternoon in January of 1989 at the former site of Boston State College right up the street from Northeastern on Huntington

Avenue. The small campus bordered the Fens and it was a five-minute walk to Melvin Hall. My second wife, Robin, our son, Hank, and Kemp were in attendance to see me "walk" as I received my degree. I completed much of the final paper over a series of weekends in Rumney, New Hampshire, where Kemp and his husband, Bill, have a cabin in the mountains. I must admit that there was a fair amount of adult beverages along with what Kemp and I commonly call 'books' to help pass the time, and stimulate my thinking.

In the early 1990s, Jerry Katz, the Bowen Principal, gave me the responsibility of being the school's lead teacher. In this role, I was bringing support to the daily operation of the building, and responsible for any matters around students and faculty. On one occasion for each of the three years that I was in the role, Jerry was away for an entire week, at what I would later learn was a retreat for the district's principals. I forget if I taught my classes, or a substitute was provided for the five days. What I remember most is sitting in Jerry's office and feeling a sense of pride that I belonged in that seat. It was a largely uneventful week, but the responsibility reinforced and made stronger the fact that I wanted to be a building Principal.

I did take the opportunity those weeks to spend time in all of my colleague's classrooms. From Kindergarten through sixth grade and including my "special" colleagues who taught art, music, and library skills, I got to see what *great* teaching looks like. How the skills in kindergarten led to a foundation for greater understanding in each ensuing year. The personal connections that were made with each student to help each access their learning. I saw and heard attention and momentum strategies in the language of my colleagues. I heard clear learning outcomes expressed, in most instances, multiple times in a lesson. Specialists referenced the current events in the students' classroom (English, math, science, social studies) to activate and connect learning. Now, I don't know if it was intentional or just a part of what had become the culture, but I heard, "FOHGYCB" out loud as a teacher responded to a child's learning more than once.

Four years later, after eighteen years of teaching elementary PE, the school district decided to change its model to a K-5, 6-8, 9-12 alignment. All the sixth and fifth graders would be moving to a feeder middle school, along with many of their teachers from those elementary schools, myself included. I thought this would be a great opportunity to teach middle school PE. To work with the 'next-up' age group in a looping opportunity. Looping means that a teacher stays with their students as they move from one grade to the next. In moving about a mile away to Brown Middle, I would already know a significant number of students from Bowen who were moving too, along with Bowen students already attending Brown.

My colleague Michael and I had just finished doing a presentation about *Respect for Difference* sponsored by the PTA of one of the elementary schools in the district. As folks were extending their praises to us both for an engaging two-hour Tuesday evening gathering, a short man wearing a sport jacket, glasses, and a bow tie at the neck of his light blue shirt, approached me.

"Hi, Hank. My name is Murph Shapiro. I'm the Principal of the new Oak Hill Middle School, opening this September. Have you applied for the Assistant Principal position?"

Oak Hill Middle School was to be the new and fourth middle school in Newton. It would be housed in what was previously a former elementary school, bearing the same name. And it was directly across the street from Brown Middle School. I would later find out that this was the only place in the country that had two, separate standing middle schools side-by-side.

During the prior three years teaching PE at Brown, I had, in addition to my regular teaching job, taken on the role of an Adjunct Instructor for co-leading a district wide professional development entitled, *Active Anti-Racism and Effective Classroom Practices for All Students.* The course was designed by two well-known scholars in the New England area and nationwide. The work of the clinical psychologist and then Mount Holyoke Professor, Dr. Beverly Daniel-Tatum, focused on racial identity development and its impact on academic achievement. Her work was combined with that of Dr. Jonathan Saphier in *The Skillful Teacher.* The course provided the framework for the curriculum that was offered to ten surrounding school districts. Dr. Tatum, in the near, future would become the President of Spelman College, while Dr. Saphier's work expanded to become and include, *Teachers Twenty-One.*

The goal that the Superintendent had set over a decade ago—to raise the academic achievement of African American students—was very much active in its pursuit of diversity equity and equality for the increasingly diverse population of students in the district. This diversity includes, but is not limited to, identities of gender, religion, sexual orientation, unique learning styles, or those whose first language is not English. The seemingly narrow focus on one group of students brings a benefit to everyone. The late Elijah Cummings said of diversity, "It is not a problem. It is our promise."

Honestly, I hadn't been thinking much at all about the new middle school and the opportunity to become an administrator. The deadline to apply was the coming Friday. But when I answered Murph Shapiro's question with, "No."

He immediately replied, "Please do." I did, and the rest, as the saying goes, is history. I was appointed to one of the Assistant Principal positions at the new middle school. I had now *gone over to the other side.*

"Aww, Hank," my colleagues began teasing me, "don't know if we should be talking around you now, an administrator. You've gone over to the other side." It was all in good fun.

I got to continue teaching the professional development graduate course that was offered to multiple districts who had formed a collaborative—Empowering Multicultural Initiatives (EMI)—toward a common goal of raising the academic achievement of all students in their respective communities. When my mentor, Bunny Meyer, the Principal of one of our feeder schools, asked me if there was something I would like to do, I replied, "Coach the basketball team." And for the first three years as an Assistant Principal at Oak Hill Middle School, I did that too. Being a basketball coach brought some great yesterdays.

AN UNIMAGINABLE TRAGEDY

$\mathcal{I}$t was late February of 2001. I had decided back in September that it was time to let go of the coaching reins but continued to lead the course and do other presentations for EMI, about racial identity and academic achievement. Winter break (the third week in February) was about to end and the calendar turning to March gave a ray of hope that the snow and cold weather would soon go away, only to return in several months. New England weather is truly unique as evidenced by having a snow day (and no school) in May of '76, the Blizzard of '78, and the April Fools Blizzard of '97; all of which I'd survived along with other hearty folks.

Upon returning from our February break, our school's music teacher sent out a greeting to everyone that included a request for anyone interested in helping with the chaperoning of the school's band who had been invited to perform in Nova Scotia, Canada. I went right to my calendar with intent to make myself available, only to find that for the Friday departure date, I already had a commitment. I'd have to pass on the opportunity.

About the middle of March every year, someone on the faculty could be heard saying, "Isn't it time for a snow day?" Sometimes all of the five days built into the school calendar for *snow days* had been used by the time St. Patrick's Day rolled around. And sometimes, the snow had begun to pile up as early as the first week of November.

Regardless, the time between winter break (in February) and spring break (in April) seemed like the longest stretch of time without any days off from school. Thus, the dreamy request for a *snow day* at this time of year was almost a guarantee. However, the Spring of 2001 would soon turn out to be a difficult time for us all at Oak Hill, and it had nothing to do with snow.

Brown, the separate standing middle school in the district directly across the street from ours, presented the perfect opportunity for many close friendships to develop between students in both schools. This became clear for us all to see when the sudden loss of a student (an asthma episode while sleeping had claimed Joy's young life) made it necessary for our guidance counselors to be available to our neighbors for student and faculty support, just across the street. I didn't know Joy personally, but she was part of our district's 400+ students who were in the METCO Program. Since its founding in 1966, during the peak of the Civil Rights Movement, the program has enrolled tens of thousands of Boston students of color in suburban districts (like Newton) in this voluntary integration opportunity. I would find out and observe that Joy's passing had a profound impact on the twenty-plus students at our school who also resided in Boston. Those who knew her well were brave and courageous enough to attend her funeral. Our counselors were there for them too.

Just before our spring break in April, the 8th grade counselor came into my office and quietly closed the door behind her. That was always a sign to me that something serious was going on. Anna, a brilliant 8th grade student with a passion for reading, had been diagnosed with lung cancer. You'd never know it by observing Anna, always smiling, and looking forward to Story Time. This daily activity was offered by our school librarian, Aaron, for students who wanted a bit of peace and quiet (away from the ruckus in the cafeteria), to hear a story while eating their lunch. Aaron's idea of Story Time at lunch was almost always well attended by students across grade levels.

The week after April spring break, our school's music teacher prepared the band for its upcoming trip. All were enthusiastic about traveling and participating in the special program in Nova Scotia, Canada at week's end. One 8th grader, Melissa whom I had known since elementary school, sought me out during her lunch time to give me a t-shirt before the group departed. A funny child who was always trying to play practical jokes on me. She'd often approach me with "Hey, Mr. Van. Bet you can't…" Or "Mr. Van, why do you …" And then go into some ungodly story that had me laughing when she was done. All with a straight face.

The motor-coach bus left the front of Oak Hill late Thursday afternoon the 26th, for the trip to Nova Scotia, Canada.

I arose at 5 AM and climbed out of bed on the morning of the 27th, thankful that we'd made it through another week. As I did each morning, I showered then turned on the news to hear the weather and traffic, so I'd be ready for the day. Fridays were dress-down days at school, and I had already ironed my jeans, my Homestead GRAYS Negro League jersey, and matching *kicks* for the day ahead. I heard the newscaster say, "Repeating our top story. A bus, carrying middle school students to a concert in Nova Scotia, crashed overnight. At this time, we know there were fatalities as reports are coming in. We'll stay on top of this breaking story as it continues to unfold."

I stopped what I was doing, grabbed the phone from the wall and called Murph.

"Was that our bus?" Was all I could get out.

His reply on the other end was a somber, "Yes."

"I'll be at school in forty-five minutes." I told Murph before hanging up.

One of the ironic parts of this tragedy, a trauma I feel to this day, is that in October of that school year, our Crisis Team had trained for exactly this scenario—the loss of a student—as part of a district wide professional development for each school's crisis team. There was a plan in place to manage such a tragedy that included school personnel, city services and a local hospital, Newton-Wellesley Hospital, who would provide much needed medical and mental health services. Remaining hydrated to deal with trauma of this magnitude saw bottles of water appearing in each classroom, provided by the school's PTA. That training was for one child. We knew that number was higher.

After a quick change into suit and tie, I arrived at school to learn that there was confirmation of four fatalities, the names of which were not yet being released. Murph and The Crisis Team, of which I was a member, met to determine how to inform the faculty and formed four notification teams. Each team included an administrator, guidance counselor, team teacher, and a member of the clergy. This was a part of our Crisis Team planning, but something none of us imagined we'd ever have to do. The task of each team was to confirm for the parents that their child would not be coming home. It remains the *hardest* thing I have had to do in my life.

Melissa. Kayla. Greg. Steven. May you rest in peace.

The sun was shining as I got into a car with my three colleagues to make the short drive to the home of Steven's parents. But the sunshine did not bring the warmth and brightness it was intended to bring that Friday morning.

The four of us entered Steven's home and were politely ushered into the living room area by his mother Elaine and her husband Bill. I was practicing with myself how I would manage to say what needed to be said. "Elaine, it has been confirmed that Steven will not be coming home." Were the words I found. I'd known Elaine and her children—Danny, Sarah, and Steven—for close to ten years while I was teaching PE at the Bowen School.

After a pause that felt more than brief, she raised her head, looked at me and said something to the effect of, "I know, Hank. He's not been answering his phone. Somehow, moms just know. I appreciate your kindness."

After returning to school from my *notification* with Elaine and Bill, the Superintendent and Murph formed another team—an administrator (myself), guidance counselor (Donna), team teacher (Butch)—to accompany a group of parents of the survivors on a flight to Canada to bring our students home, including the deceased. Jimmy, one of the district Assistant Superintendents, gave me ten, one hundred dollar bills in an envelope before leaving Newton for any expenses, food and the like, which we might incur. We left school around noontime and headed to a nearby municipal airport to board a plane in the early afternoon for the trip. The customs process moved quickly (we were going to another country) and we boarded a twin engine plane for the trip to Nova Scotia. We received a heads-up from the pilot that there was a large media presence awaiting our arrival. After landing, the pilot parked the plane away from the media frenzy I could see in the distance, and ground transportation met us on the tarmac. It was no more than twenty steps from the plane to the bus that would take us to the hospital where the surviving students awaited our arrival. Fortunately, we didn't have any interaction with the assembled crowd at that time. When we arrived at the hospital, we were ushered in through a private entrance to avoid the assembled crowd.

Students are resilient. Their outward expressions when I saw them sitting in chairs huddled together in a private wing of the hospital, each holding a teddy bear provided by the hospital, did not indicate the trauma that each had lived through only a few hours earlier. While enroute overnight, the bus driver misjudged his speed going around a highway exit, causing the bus to flip on its side and roll over, ejecting four students, all who lost their lives in this tragic event. There were students at each grade level amongst the victims who now were dealing with the unthinkable, the sudden loss of close friends. There were two or three others who received minor injuries, one required crutches to walk.

I soon found myself on my way to a press conference with one of the hospital's doctors who was in charge of caring for our students. Before it began, I called my son Hank to tell him how much I loved him, then gathered myself before facing the questions.

Later that evening, we returned home on a 727 jet that someone in Newton who knew someone, who knew someone in commercial aviation arranged to have the aircraft available for the needs of the situation. At the airfield, the four hearses were kept out of sight from us. But after boarding the aircraft, I could hear the distinct sound of each coffin being loaded below. I'm sure others did too.

Once in the air, as I looked out over the night sky at the city lights below, a range of emotions flooded my every thought. Our school had lost four students, but four sets of parents had lost a child. The landing was bumpy for us all; parents, their children, and I heard the coffins bounce when the jet touched down. It was about 3 AM

Saturday morning. As we boarded a bus, I saw in the darkness four hearses almost out of sight, waiting to provide their service, one for each coffin. It was almost 4 AM on Saturday when the bus carrying us arrived back to the Oak Hill Middle School. When I stepped off, the first thing I noticed, even in the darkness of night illuminated only by streetlights and those on the building's exterior, were the countless hearts and messages written by students in chalk all along the sidewalk, in tribute to their four classmates. I went inside to drop off some items, gather my belongings, and drove home.

My time up to then, was consumed with grieving students, colleagues, parents, and family. Later I did take the rare private time alone to do my own grieving. Still operating on adrenaline, I took a short rest and went back out to get a haircut and stop by Kemp's home in Cambridge. Sitting at the dining room table, I noticed the daily Boston Herald newspaper with the headline telling of the accident and showing the overturned bus with students sitting on the grass nearby. Instruments and paper were strewn everywhere on the grass in the photo. I screamed and began to sob uncontrollably. Kemp, who had gone to the second floor of his home, came rushing downstairs and just held me tight, yet lovingly, until I finally was able to stop and compose myself.

The wakes and funerals began that Sunday and concluded on Thursday of the following week. Funeral in the AM. A wake in the afternoon. Repeat. My colleague and fellow administrator, Bev, held my hand, and I hers, wherever we went during those yesterdays that seemed like they would never end.

A community wide memorial service was held outdoors at our school. Large tents were set up on the athletic field to protect folks from the hot sun, and chairs were arranged to seat the entire school population; parents and community members facing a stage and lectern. The media was respectful of the moment, including not having any cameras in helicopters flying overhead. During the memorial, then Mayor, David Cohen, said something that has stayed with me to this day whenever I must navigate a difficult situation. "Out of something *so* bad, will come something *good!*"

Elaine and her husband Bill have created The Steve Glidden Foundation. Its website reads, "SGF's mission is to make a difference in the lives of children who are homeless, refugees, or exposed to violence or abuse. Each summer, through the SGF Summer Camp Scholarship Program, dozens of children are able to benefit from the same enriching summer camp experiences that the more fortunate among us simply take for granted. This opportunity can be nothing short of transformational, both for the children and for their parents or caregivers." Out of something *so* bad yesterday, have come many *tomorrows* for the now hundreds of young people who have benefitted from the foundation in Steven's name. They have also fought tirelessly to bring about legislation to require seat belts for students riding in school buses and motor coaches.

The Royal Canadian Mounted Police sent nine members to represent Canada, all in full-dress uniform, and an engraved stone bearing the names of the four students. The gift from the people of Nova Scotia, was permanently placed at the school's entrance.

We were less than two weeks from the Massachusetts Comprehensive Assessment System (MCAS), the state-wide exams at each grade. Although a "waiver request" was submitted by our district following the tragedy, the State denied our request, and planning for the administering of these assessments continued.

Sometime in May, I received an invitation for two from a local organization that was planning a trip in early June to Washington,

DC, for the families associated with the tragedy. After a little checking, I was honored to accept the invite. It was a gorgeous day when my wife Robin and I arrived at the municipal airport for our two-hour flight from Hanscom Field in Bedford. The same airport where we had taken off and landed only weeks ago. The highlight of the trip for me was a self-guided tour of the Holocaust Museum. My emotions were still close to the surface anyway, and I wasn't quite prepared for the feelings I would experience during those hours.

In the museum, there was a boxcar. I'll never forget walking the width to its center, pausing at its midpoint, then walking from end to end while taking in all of what was around me. The stories of those who had passed the same way, but without their freedom, so many yesterdays ago.

We came around one corner and there on our left were thousands of shoes that stretched further than I can remember. I had never smelled death before. But as I walked the corridor I knew the smell permeating the air was the scent of death-of dead bodies.

Yet another passage took us through what at first appeared to be a family room of portraits on either side of the walkway. Suddenly, as if we were walking out of a garage, we entered a space where the side walls were covered by family portraits all the way to the ceiling—all different, all unique in the story that each told.

In early June, Anna succumbed to the disease destroying her body. We had another child to lay to rest. Rest in peace, Anna.

TAKING A LEAP OF FAITH

The following year, on a sunny, Friday afternoon, another dress down day (I had on a pair of jeans, my Kansas City Monarch Negro League jersey and matching sneakers), my administrative assistant, Doreen, poked her head into my office to say that the Superintendent was on the phone and wanted to speak with me.

"Hey, Jeff. How are you and the family?"

"We're all well. Thanks for asking. How about you?"

"It's a two-star day," I replied. "It's Friday and the eagle flies today."

"What flies?" He quizzically asked.

"The eagle flies. It's payday."

"Okay, Hank. I'm catching on now. Listen, I need to see you later today after dismissal."

All kinds of thoughts are now going through my mind because, well, if the Superintendent summons you to his office, what could this be about? I drove fifteen-minutes across the city to arrive at the Education Center for the district. Walking down the hallway to his office, some folks remarked "Nice jersey, Hank. But who are the Monarchs?" I'd take a few moments to educate those who were not familiar with the history and story of the Negro Leagues. Prohibited from playing major league baseball until Jackie Robinson broke the color line in 1947, their stories are often lost or stolen from the history of the game.

"Hi, Hank. Go on in. Jeff's waiting for you," Mary, his administrative assistant, greeted me as I walked in the door.

"Love that jersey," were Jeff's first words. "But you have to tell me who the Monarchs are" Another opportunity to gladly pay it forward.

What followed next was totally unexpected.

"Hank, the Williams Elementary School Principal is leaving after this year, and I'd like to offer you the job of Interim Principal there, for the upcoming school year." I certainly wasn't expecting that!

"Whoa." I paused and exhaled, "Tell me more."

Jeff proceeded to share with me what he could about the situation, and outlined the transition for me, including being introduced to the community at an evening meeting the following week.

"Yes, yes. And yes. The only request I have is that I take the weekend to talk this over with my wife." When I got home later that afternoon and shared my news with Robin, she gave her excited and full support of me grasping this great chance to advance my career.

"Of course. Give me a call on Monday. This is a great opportunity for you and when I mentioned it to Murph, he didn't hesitate to give you a full endorsement for being able to do this job. *'He's ready'* were his exact words."

I called Jeff on Monday to accept and later that week I was introduced to the Williams community as the Interim Principal for the upcoming school year. The school was located closer to my home in West Newton and made the daily commute shorter. The closer location allowed me to get there *quick, fast, and in a hurry,* especially on a couple of weekends when the building alarm inexplicably began sounding. I rushed over and was greeted by the local authorities and used my passcode to turn off the alarm. Such is the life of a Principal.

OUT OF SOMETHING VERY BAD, COMES SOMETHING VERY GOOD

The next spring, I applied for the position that I was in as Interim. But was not chosen for the position. Didn't even get an interview. Through the grapevine, it came back to me that because my background was in middle school, the selection committee was looking for a leader who had experience in elementary school teaching and learning. I guess all of the eighteen years that I had spent working at elementary schools in the district, was overlooked in considering my candidacy.

It was a difficult pill (rejection) to swallow, particularly when the person chosen for the role (a colleague from another district I'd known for a number of years) sought me out to inquire, "Hank, what's going on here? I'm surprised that you were not chosen." I shared my thoughts. Not earning the position would see me returning to Oak Hill Middle School in my previous role of Assistant Principal.

In the fall of the next school year, Murph announced his retirement would be in June. Finding his replacement began with the job posting and would stretch out into the winter months, and the new Principal was announced in the spring.

One afternoon, as the deadline for applying for the position was approaching, I was finishing a write up on my computer for a teacher observation I had done. This part of my job was one that I looked forward to doing. It afforded me the opportunity to build relationships with my colleagues and move away from being *the evaluator* to *another learner,* in their classroom space. The labor-intensive work began with a pre-observation conference where my colleague would outline their learning objectives for the lesson. I'd always ask if there was something specific that they wanted me to provide feedback on, in addition to the repertoires of teaching I'd be observing. Following the observation, the two of us would have a pre-scheduled post observation conference. I'd get my write-ups back to each within a week's time. The district's collectively bargained four year process meant that some individuals would have three observations (these were the teachers who had not yet gained *Professional Teaching Status*), others two, still others only one, and still others just a personal goal meeting. As someone tasked with the supervision and observation of fifteen or more colleagues, my capacity for practicing good time management came in handy. One post observation conference still stands out for me.

My colleague was an experienced teacher, one I had a lot of respect for, because they knew how to get students' attention and maintain it, all the while making personal connections with each during class time and beyond. During the observation, my colleague posed a question for each to share their response to. "What is something that you are proud of?" There were no more than twelve students seated in a semicircle. As each student told a short story of what they were proud of, I noticed a pattern taking place. None of the three students of color in the class gave a response. At the post observation conference, I asked my colleague if they had noticed this too. There was a pregnant pause. "No, Hank. I didn't notice." They went on to say something to the effect of, "I have to do better in that regard. Thanks for bringing that to my attention." *That's* why this was a part of my job that I enjoyed. Paying-it-forward, not evaluating.

Murph stepped into my office and said, "Have you applied for the Principal position here?" And, honestly, just like six years previous when he asked me an almost identical question, I hadn't been thinking much at all about being the next Principal at Oak Hill Middle School. This, despite the obvious fact that doing so would provide the opportunity to advance my ongoing goal of becoming not only an administrator, but a building Principal—not *interim*.

"I've considered it a bit." I said as I turned away from the computer screen and gave him my full attention.

"You should. You don't want to work for someone else when that someone can be you."

I submitted my application ahead of the deadline and was notified of the next steps in the process. This included a personal essay that addressed the district's four core values: effective communication, centrality of the classroom, respect for human differences, practice collegiality.

The first interview came on a weekday evening and was held at the Education Center. In the conference room, the large, oblong shaped table sat five people on one side, and five on the other side. I was ushered in and sat at one end, and the Superintendent at the opposite head. The group represented a cross section of *constituents*—teachers, parents, district department heads, assistant superintendent. It was just a bit *intimidating*. I sat straight up and got comfortable in my seat for the questions that followed for the next sixty minutes or so, some of which came from the essay I had written.

The second interview was the following day with the school's faculty during a scheduled faculty meeting time. A concern that became a theme in their questions for me was about holding students accountable for inappropriate behavior. There were others that came from the questions from my essay. I guess folks wanted to see if I was consistent and had a discipline plan they could endorse.

The following day was one of two *visiting days* by the other two candidates. This required me to be out of the building. Lastly, I met with my colleague, Carolyn (the assistant superintendent for curriculum and instruction), and Jeff, the district's superintendent. I was so nervous that I was noticeably sweating about halfway through our forty-five-minute meeting.

I got a call that spring evening from Jeff, to offer me the Principalship at Oak Hill Middle School. The indescribable feelings I experienced at that moment was a yesterday that I'll never forget.

THE SEAL CRAWL

The four minutes between each fifty-minute class period was a rush hour of student traffic, like in Penn Station, moving from one room to the next. Or from one part of the building to the other end by using the several stairwells.

On certain days, at certain times I'd position myself just outside of the main office to help direct traffic during these moments of orchestrated chaos.

"Stay to the right going up!"

"Stay to the left coming down!"

"Do you have an elevator pass?"

"I'm just holding her books." A student with crutches to support them from a leg injury nodded in affirmation, with a smile directed my way.

"Oh, so as the helper, you get to ride, too?" I asked the book carrier.

"Yeah, that's right Mr. Van." Without looking me in the eye.

These confusing yet orderly transitions took place in stairwells multiple times each day. They increased in intensity as midday approached, which brought lunch time with it. The expectation was that traversing around the building was to be done by *walking*. And sometimes, a student, usually a sixth grader on their way to lunch, forgot and their attempt at *fast walking* quickly turned into an all-out sprint. When I caught someone running, I'd have the student walk back to the end of the hallway and retrace their steps by walking. If I knew you as a repeat offender, then the two of us would walk back to the end of the hallway, and together do a *seal crawl* on the carpeted floor back to the entrance of the cafeteria. What's a *seal crawl*? It's an exercise I would often do when teaching elementary PE that starts out by lying down on the floor with your hands under your shoulders in a push-up position, then extending your arms while your toes and feet contact the floor behind you. Then, as does a *seal*, you use just your hands and arms to move along with your feet dragging behind you. There was always an audience that provided laughter and some gentle teasing directed at the student who was "caught speeding," as the offender and myself navigated the hallway. It was fun and the students enjoyed watching, avoiding being caught, and joining. I found it as a way of further connecting with students.

"Mr. Van, I can't go any further!" Would occasionally be the exclamation.

"Can you do three more?" I'd ask.

"I can only do two."

"Okay, let's do it," and the student would gleefully, yet somewhat exhausted, rise to their feet and walk to their destination.

One day, soon after I had been appointed to be the next Principal for Oak Hill, I was in the hallway as lunch time was about to begin, feeling somewhat like a police officer manning a speed trap, as the first wave of students began to flow by. Suddenly, here came one of my repeat offenders speeding down the hallway. I put my hand up, made a circle motion with a finger and pointed back to the end of the hallway. As I'd done in the past, I accompanied the student back down the hallway and together we did the *seal crawl* as a few students, holding their laughter, watched on, along with another smiling adult (a Teacher Assistant), before the student rose triumphantly and headed into the cafeteria.

Later that afternoon following dismissal, I got a call from Mary, Jeff's administrative assistant.

"Hold on a moment, Hank. Jeff needs to speak to you."

After a moment of small talk, he got to the point of his call. Apparently, the student had gone home and told their mother about the incident. She had called Jeff and, using an irate tone, told him to investigate the matter because it was her intention to go to the news media about my unacceptable behavior. And she would be filing a civil lawsuit alleging that I had violated her son's civil rights. She had described me as standing over her son and demanded that he finish to the entrance of the cafeteria.

Shocked at what I was hearing, there was a long pause and he then asked me to describe to him what had transpired. I did, with all the details above and including that there was an adult witness to the event.

Another pause.

"You're not going to continue this practice, right?"

I took his query to be more of an order, not a request, that would not be violated in the future.

"No, won't be doing that again." I replied in candor.

"One more thing," Jeff stated before our conversation ended. "Don't say anything to anyone and do not respond to anything that is written or said about you or this incident in the media."

"I can do that." This would turn out to be easier said than done. The student's mother proceeded to lambast my character by writing *"Someone who is from New York would never treat a child in such a way,"* in an op-ed published in the local newspaper, They would also call for my license to be revoked, and filed a suit under the state's anti-discrimination laws stating I had violated their child's civil rights.

The story was all over the local news; one headline read, "School Administrator verbally and physically harassed student." Friends from out of state started reaching out to hear my side of what had happened. For a couple of days, news team began appearing outside of our schoolhouse at dismissal time. I observed some students being interviewed and then demonstrating what the *seal crawl* looked like for the news camera on the sidewalk.

I remembered Jeff's cautionary utterance, "Don't say anything to anyone." I did, however, address the faculty about the incident should they hear students talking about it as the suit was filed.

Nothing happened during the summer months as I prepared myself and my admin team (Ken, Bev, and Suzanne) for the upcoming school year. In mid-August, I received notification from the state that the case was being dismissed as no violation of civil rights had occurred and there was no grounds to revoke my license. Following the incident and into the next school year, whenever I'd see that parent, they'd approach me with smiles and little chit chat that had nothing to do with the incident, as if nothing had happened.

"Don't say anything to anyone."

I began our first faculty meeting at the end of August by informing every one of the state's decision. The cloud was lifted. I could turn my full focus on working with an amazing faculty to create a community of learners to support the work of students and teachers every day.

Starting with all the adults in the building, we began the process of identifying then developing a Mission Statement and accompanying Core Values. We planned for a session where the task outlined was to discuss and offer input and collect it from everyone in attendance. Small groups worked for forty-five minutes before reassembling. Colleagues from across disciplines volunteered to collate the responses, put them into general categories, and at the ensuing faculty gathering, present their work and ask for additional feedback. At the monthly School Council meeting, feedback from parents on the draft documents was sought.

I found a good degree of pride when I recently looked at the current student handbook for the Oak Hill Middle School. The words we authored over a decade ago remain there, as the light house we envisioned for our schoolhouse in those yesterdays. Inside the handbook reads:

Oak Hill Middle School, a community of learners, holds firm to the belief that learning is incremental and therefore, all children can learn. Smart is something that you get, not something that you are! Children will develop at varying rates and each has their own unique learning style. It is our intent to support the learning of all children by nurturing a sense of confidence to promote effective effort in our community that allows each child to find their learning zone – a place where one can be successful and feel good about oneself. With this in mind, children will be able to take realistic and challenging risks that will lead them to further academic and social development. The diagram below expresses these beliefs.

Additionally, the Mission and Core Values statements created by the entire community continue to provide the same guidance and direction we envisioned.

That is a yesterday which feels *I-wanna-puff-out-my-chest* great.

These read:

<u>Mission</u>: *The essential mission of Oak Hill Middle School focuses on raising the academic achievement of all students and nurturing their growth and development. We believe that:*

- *Learning is incremental.*
- *Each of our students is capable of achieving at a high level.*
- *Effort and effective strategies are the key for success.*
- *Collaboration/collegiality removes obstacles to our mission.*
- *Nurture curiosity, creativity, and a passion for learning.*
- *Foster self-confidence and success for all learners.*

<u>Core Values</u>:

Respect for Human Differences - We expect our community members to demonstrate:

- *Respect for themselves, others and the property we share.*
- *Respect for the contribution of each individual.*
- *Respect for the responsibility of giving back to the community. At Oak Hill, we take care of ourselves, others, and the environment.*

Academic Achievement /Thinking Skills - We expect our students to:

- *Stretch themselves beyond their comfort zone and Find Out How Good You Can Be every day.*
- *Demonstrate their willingness to take responsibility for their own learning.*

- *Use their acquired skills to engage in:*
    - ❋ *Thoughtful research by organizing information.*
    - ❋ *Technology literacy.*
    - ❋ *Clear communication.*
    - ❋ *Creative thinking.*
    - ❋ *Appreciation for the arts.*

I remember the last edit made to the document was *appreciation for the arts*. Not surprisingly, when the entire group was asked, "What is missing?" It was a teacher in this discipline who pointed out they did not see their curriculum represented. It was a teachable moment for me on the path toward equity and inclusion.

These words had to come off the page and become living for our schoolhouse. I devoted time in my initial address to students each September to say out loud our mission and vision say in the Handbook. I asked each teacher to have a conversation with their respective classes, using the following open and honest question: What do we want our classroom to look like?

Here is a sample of what we were able to do in the months and years that followed, under the guidance of our mission and vision:

- Eliminated the lowest level of math in the 7th and 8th grade, which raised the floor for low achieving math students and increased student achievement.
- Established professional learning communities which allowed for cross discipline conversation and communication about student achievement and teaching practices.
- Created a Reading Team, and designed a three-year action plan to integrate reading strategies across discipline areas and improve reading scores in a high achieving school house.

- Focus on examining the way we teach our students to answer "open response questions" on standardized tests.
- Promoted equity and an appreciation of diversity by enlisting teachers, students, and parents in making *respect* the cornerstone of what happens in the schoolhouse.

The last point, *making respect a cornerstone,* is a reflection of the concern that I had heard during the interview process from teachers and staff.

One year, a school dance with a DJ on a Friday evening, had the theme of the Oscars. Complete with a red carpet to enter the redecorated-for-the-occasion cafeteria and included figurine shaped prizes. Seeing our students taking on the persona of various famous movie stars was a sight to behold. It gave me what author, Emily Style, refers to as windows and mirrors—those experiences where I can see myself reflected in the lives of others. I found my thoughts going back to the yesterdays of my time in those choir shows. And if you've never attended a middle school dance, well let's say it's interesting to watch the social interactions of all different kinds of students. Some you can predict. Others will take you completely by surprise. The joy of being in that moment remains special.

I had heard it said that as a Principal, it is important to have a positive relationship with your school's Head Custodian. Tom and I had worked together for a period since the school opened in 1997. He'd tell me along the way that he really liked the way that I worked with students, including his granddaughter. In fact, he shared that me being there was one of the reasons he chose to have her attend Oak Hill. Sometimes, his granddaughter, Katie, wasn't the easiest person to get along with but she had a kind heart when letting her guard down. I remember going to a few of her basketball or soccer games on weekends.

"Mr. Van. *What* are you doing here? Oh, I'm so embarrassed."

"I came to see you play. I told you I would, and here I am."

"Oh, I'm so embarrassed."

One day in late fall as the temperatures went down and the colorful leaves of New England had all but fallen from their trees, Tom sought me out while I was in the hallway. When we met outside the main office during the first period, he had a concerned look on his face.

"Can you smell that?"

I paused for a moment, took an inhale of the air in the hallway immediately outside of the main office and could clearly sense an increasing odor of oil.

"Oil. I can smell oil."

"It's coming from the boiler. I've called it in. We may have to evacuate the building."

This was an eerie moment for me. Only weeks before, during our Crisis Team meeting, the scenario we had table-planned for and practiced was the evacuation of the building, traversing to a safe shelter (Brown Middle School across the street,) and the potential for a chaotic dismissal if parents needed to pick up their child. I felt myself right back at living out the planning of the crisis for the loss of a student's life.

I contacted the district office to appraise them about the situation and assembled the Crisis Team to quickly review the plan we had prepared. By this time, the smell of oil was beginning to permeate through the entire building. Second floor teachers were calling the office to say they could smell oil. The first fire company arrived. Soon the Superintendent wanted to know about our plan and how he could help. He told me it was my call for what to do. When the local police appeared, I handed over *command* to both the fire and police. This was part of the training. What followed next, though, was as close to organized chaos as I've ever had to experience as a Principal.

Brown was contacted and our students would go to their auditorium.

We evacuated the building.

All students were accounted for in the Brown auditorium.

Parents, via robo-call, were contacted about the situation.

A decision was made to contact the bus company for an early dismissal of our students. Brown's schedule was about thirty minutes behind ours.

Parents began showing up in-mass to pick up their child, each of whom had to be accounted for. The system for doing this, untested in real time and sketchy at best, worked as intended. Each child was accounted for.

The fire department found the nexus of the leak and fixed the problem, and the building was in the process of being *aired out* with open windows and multiple fans strategically placed in hallways.

School buses began showing up for our early dismissal.

Parents had to park a ways away and were now walking in to pick up their child *and* one or two of their friends whom the child's parents had given permission for picking up on such an occasion. This was part of the registration process all schools go through—who can pick up their child if they were not able.

All students were accounted for.

Brown would be dismissed in about an hour, which meant more school buses and more parents would be descending on the already controlled, chaotic scene.

I felt like being in one of those glass snow globes that you shake and wait for the snowflakes to settle, only to have someone else shake the whole thing again.

By the time Brown was dismissing its students, all our students were accounted for and had been safely picked up, handed off to another parent, or boarded their bus in time before the second dismissal time. What a yesterday.

B.R.I.M.

I began to follow the work and research of the National Association of Secondary Principals (N.A.S.S.Ps.). The organization's work led "a process of self-evaluation, collaboration across disciplines, to create common assessments within disciplines, and examining student work to inform instruction." The work had the acronym B.R.I.M. which stood for Breaking Ranks in the Middle. I shared some of these articles and research with my middle school colleagues John, Gina, and Todd; and we started up a conversation about *rethinking* middle school in our district. An impetus for us to undertake this task was that depending on which middle school you attended, your experience could vary greatly from another on the other side of town. For example, not all world languages were taught at each school. Not all the middle schools had the same schedule, which limited the possibilities for sharing faculty and program, as well as in-district faculty development.

N.A.S.S.P. was planning a multi-day professional development to be held in Virginia during the summer. The three of us registered, attended, began our planning, and came home like the South Carolina Women's Basketball Team comes out of halftime after hearing inspirational words from their coach, Dawn Staley..

When the new school year began, we met multiple times with our assistant superintendent, Brenda, where we outlined our plan to *rethink middle school* guided by the research of B.R.I.M. over the next twelve plus months. We had an eye to two years of preparation for bringing about the changes, especially in the schedule. We knew that the bus schedules often drive the starting and dismissal times for our schools, so getting the four schools on as close to an identical schedule was going to be a *huge* mountain to climb. Putting that aside, but still on the front burner, we looked to the programmatic changes where resources could be shared. Invariably, though, we found ourselves coming back to the dilemma of the bus schedule which kept getting in the way. John (Principal at Brown, directly across the street from us) and I thought long and hard about how we could do simultaneous arrivals and dismissals. We even consulted with a city planning engineer and the person in charge of the district's school buses, about traffic flow and pedestrian safety to try and overcome this obstacle. The four of us had made a little progress in sharing resources based largely on location with one another. We continued meeting with Brenda, to keep her appraised and seek any advice from her or other members of the central staff.

Following the February break, the four of us were ushered to an unexpected meeting we *thought* would be to further explain our progress and next steps toward our goal of next year's September, still eighteen-plus months in the future. In attendance with Brenda were several of the district's curriculum heads *and* the master scheduler for the district.

I don't remember the person's name, probably because when given the floor to speak that person spoke and informed the four of us that we had to accelerate our plan to implement it for the next school year in September, *seven* months away.

There was silence that was palpable and a gaze of astonishment, disbelief and *wtf* seemed to appear on our four faces at the same time.

I lowered my chin to my chest, closed my eyes, scratched the back of my head, and said, "This shit ain't gonna work in that time frame." My words broke the silence.

"Hank, I understand your emotions," I heard as my eyes remained closed, still slowly scratching the back of my head. "But the thinking is to try out a five-day schedule in the middle schools, before implementing it on a larger scale for the two high schools, the following year." We were the guinea pigs, so to speak.

The five-day schedule was one option we had considered. We knew that *any* change of this kind would be difficult, especially when two of the schools—mine included—were operating on a six day rotating schedule.

We'd have to sell the idea to the union.

We'd have to sell the idea to the teachers.

We'd have to sell the idea to parents.

We'd have to learn a whole new scheduling system.

All of this in less than seven months.

Brenda came to a faculty meeting to sell the idea.

The union requested attending meetings and regular involvement with any decisions made. That was actually easy to do.

Current parents and some of their children wanted to know why such a change was being made.

These are yesterdays where I had to walk the line of maintaining the best interest of my teachers and their working environment, while also being in unison with the interests of the district.

The year that we tried to implement the five-day schedule was far from the best of times. Frankly, it was miserable for everyone in some way or another. Brown's proximity made it necessary for us to be out-of-sync on the schedule. Between our two schools, there were over 1400 students. Having the same arrival and dismissal time would not be feasible. I found my time being taken up, *away* from our school for longer periods of time each day. Fewer opportunities showed up in the schedule for sharing world language teachers between our two schools. There was predictable dissatisfaction among my colleagues in having to make necessary changes to the rhythm of teaching their curriculums. Whereas we previously used a number system, "Today is Day 1," now we were asking, "Is today Tuesday? Or Day 3?" Funny at times, these moments highlighted what I had said, *"This shit ain't gonna work."*

As the 100th day of school (you have got to be there to feel the pride of the moment) approached during the winter months, my attention turned to the annual excitement of welcoming the incoming sixth grade students and their parents to our community. Of greater importance to me, along with my colleagues, was what schedule changes could be made for the upcoming school year.

Soon thereafter, as the crocuses poked their colors into the sunlight, often giving a false hope that spring was about to arrive; the four of us gathered for our regularly scheduled meeting at the Education Center. Brenda announced that each school would be able to determine its own schedule for the upcoming September.

Brenda would be visiting each middle school to answer any questions from faculty. I remember her words to my colleagues in our school's library where we held faculty meetings. She followed through on her intent for transparency when speaking to everyone, "I want you all to know that Hank was the strongest pushback against the schedule change. He was thinking of the impact on you."

Yesterday.

SEE THE WORLD: MY TRIP TO CHINA

The Newton Public Schools, over time, developed an international relationship with another school in Beijing, China. In support of this partnership, each year, ten high school students and two teachers from the district would go to China for a semester of learning. At the same time, a similar sized group of students from China would attend classes in one of the district's two high schools. In addition, each year, groups of administrators (assistant superintendents, principals, curriculum, and high school department heads) were offered the opportunity to travel to China for ten days. I had the privilege to be selected to be a part of the group traveling in April of 2007. The preparation for the trip included multiple visits to the *travel clinic* at a local hospital to receive the required vaccinations, taking regular hour-long classes to learn some basic Mandarin to help us *try* to communicate with our hosts in their native tongue, and of course ensuring that passports and other documents were up to date and in order.

Our flight left Boston's Logan Airport on a somewhat chilly Thursday, April morning, headed first to Chicago for our connecting flight to Shanghai. When we landed in the Windy City, it was even colder and snow showers made the scene quite winter-like, even though the calendar said otherwise. Arriving at the gate for our thirteen-hour flight the snow continued to fall and our 11:30 departure time was pushed back while the aircraft—a 747 jumbo jet—was being de-iced. I was fidgety but excited, as I had never flown on a 747 but had heard about the upstairs amenities onboard. My thoughts returned to the yesterday of flying with my parents to the Caribbean years ago. This was post 9/11, so the thought of going up to the cockpit with the crew *probably* wasn't going to happen.

As departure time approached, the jet was de-iced a second time, and forty-five minutes later, a third time before we finally boarded almost two hours late.

This plane is huge, I thought once onboard and looking for my window seat. I found it, sat down, and started to notice right away that there weren't many folks getting on. In fact, when the announcement was made to the crew to "Prepare for departure," there was hardly anyone in the rows in front of me, behind me, or across the aisle to my right. It was almost like our traveling group of nine had the entire aircraft to ourselves. The thirteen-hour flight would take us over the north pole and Siberia, and there was plenty of room to fully stretch out for a nap on the middle row of seats adjacent to mine—which I obliged in using after watching a movie and having a meal.

It was early evening, the next day, when we arrived, two hours later than scheduled. I was awestruck that I was now on the other side of the world. I'd never been so far away from my home before. I called my wife, Robin, to say we'd safely arrived. We gathered our luggage and found our ground transportation for the thirty-minute ride to the city center, located on the country's central coast. Along the way, the motor coach drove in the center of five lanes on the highway with a speed limit of "45" periodically painted on the roadway. At one point, the driver hurriedly announced on the bus PA system that a bullet train was approaching on our right. In the short amount of time it took me to get out my camera, the train had whooshed past us in the blink of an eye.

Because we had arrived later than anticipated, we didn't go directly to the hotel, but rather to a planned evening cruise on the Huangpu River. As the bus pulled up to the pier for this first adventure, there were long lines of people waiting to board a boat for the river cruise. Somehow, someone had arranged for our group to go immediately to the front of the line. Those waiting were straining their necks for a look to see who these Americans were. At that moment, I felt like a rock star! The waterway seemed like Times Square in that there were *so* many boats on the river. We passed several colonial era buildings that had formerly been the residence of heads of state. All were lit up to shine and stood out beneath the evening's starry sky.

We didn't arrive at the Jing An Hotel until almost midnight. However, there was a meal prepared and awaiting our group when we did. At the meal, as most of my traveling colleagues comfortably used chopsticks, I found myself in the minority of asking, "May I please have a fork." I made a promise to myself right then that for the duration of the trip, I'd learn and only use the country's signature eating utensil. By the following day, I was picking up individual peas, water chestnuts, and melon from my plate using chopsticks.

The next day after breakfast (using my chopsticks), we headed out for a ride on an underground railway that traversed the Bund, which is a famed waterfront promenade that was lined with colonial era buildings. Now I could see where we had been only a few hours before.

"We need to find a bank," one of our group's members exclaimed, and several others, myself included, chimed in that we had the same need.

The Bund railway car could not hold our whole group, but we met on the other side and then headed off in search of a nearby bank. When we entered, there were at least eight lines of people waiting to be served at the window. I went to what I thought would be a quick moving queue. Of course, such wasn't the case and as I watched my friends get their funds and walk outside, it was becoming evident to me that I was going to be one of, if not the last one, to get some cash (yuan). I was prophetic in my belief about being the last, but I wasn't ready for what happened next.

When I turned away from the teller to rejoin the group, they had all moved outside. I walked out of the bank and the group was nowhere to be seen. Standing in front of the building that smoggy morning, I looked left and saw no one, save for a few pedestrians.

Same result when I looked to the right. To say that I found myself suddenly in a state of panic would be an understatement. Here I am, thousands of miles from home and I'm all alone. *At least I knew how to get back to the hotel from where I was*, I thought. I checked my pocket to be sure I had the hotel's business card with directions I'd picked up at the front counter the night before.

I walked one block to the left and peered down the street as far as I could see. No one looked familiar.

I turned to walk in the opposite direction to another corner. As I again passed the bank's entrance, I could feel my heart racing and beads of sweat bubbling up on my forehead.

"Hank! Hank!" I heard a familiar voice shout out.

A block away I could see several folks frantically waving their arms overhead to get my attention.

First, I exhaled. I quickened my steps, but rather walked with a sense of relief to meet up with the group.

"Where'd you go?" Someone asked.

I half-jokingly, yet dead seriously responded, "You mean to tell me that as the only Black person in this group, no one noticed I was not with you?" It was a light-hearted yesterday that turned out fine. But oh my God, what if they hadn't noticed.

We had scrumptious lunch in "Old Shanghai" where I continued to master my utensil skills. There were motor scooters zipping around and dodging pedestrians and other vehicles everywhere.

We visited a marketplace where I had a quick lesson in how to barter with someone, only to find several others chiming in for us to look at their goods for sale. As we walked along the crowded sidewalks, I felt a tug on my arm. It was a merchant who was still trying to make me an offer I could not refuse.

The second night while in Shanghai we went to a stage show at the Nan Shi Theatre featuring an amazing group of acrobats.

The ten women and ten men flawlessly executed multiple feats using implements that included sticks, swords, dishes, and poles while balancing atop each other or speeding around an enclosed cage on motorcycles.

The next morning, following the performance, we went directly to the airport for a short flight to HuangShan. When we arrived at our destination, it was like going from modern times back to the Middle Ages.

The residence where we stayed was a five-hundred-year-old inn that had been impeccably preserved with almost all of its original grandeur. The center of the structure was open to the sky, and I would learn that most, if not all of the buildings in China had the same feature which allowed nature in all its forms—sun, rain, wind—to grace the edifice with all the spirit of the culture.

Trays of freshly picked green tea and a pot of hot water were strategically placed and available for us. Today, whenever offered tea, I always request green tea.

During our stay at the inn, we ventured out and traversed through rice patties, where workers tended to their fields and sent a wave and a smile our way. Some owned water buffalo to help with their farming. I'd learned that the annual income for these farmers was about two-thousand US dollars.

The next morning, we boarded a bus to visit nearby Yellow Mountain. Our Newton colleagues who had been to the site told us before leaving that it was about a sixty-to-ninety-minute walk to the top. Led by our student guides, Angie and Michelle, we began our ascent just before ten in the morning. It would be a little past two in the afternoon when we finally reached the summit of the mountain. Most of the walk was up cement stairs at a steep incline. There were rest areas along the scenic pathway, and then upward and onward we went. Passing us along the route were workers carrying supplies on long bamboo poles to the stores and hotel at the top. I'd later learn that each was receiving about thirty-five cents for each round trip up and back down the mountain.

I was at the front of the group following Angie (I was not going to be left behind again) when suddenly one of the women in our group let out a shrieking yell of fear and surprise. A short-tailed Yellow Mountain monkey, standing about three feet in height, had appeared from the forest and stood right next to my startled colleague. The monkey, expecting some kind of food, was probably disappointed when not offered anything to eat. We continued on our way to the top and the monkey headed back into the forest.

"What time is it?"

"How much further do we have to go?"

Fortunately, the cool sunshine and breezy weather made our climb just a bit more bearable as we passed the noontime hour. We came into a clearing of another rest area when I noticed something whiz by and out of sight. It was a tramway.

"You mean to tell me that we could have taken that ride to the top?" Someone said in a frustrated voice. Later, after resting, having something to eat, and taking in more spectacular views, we'd end up taking the ninety-second ride (I timed it) back down the mountain. We all rested well that night after dinner.

The Xuning Middle School was not formally a part of the student exchange program. Nonetheless, Newton had built a relationship with the school and the following day we arrived in the late morning. We were first welcomed at the entrance when seeing the large, electronic announcement screen display, *Welcome visitors from afar*, then were soon greeted by the school's Principal and a few other staff members. As we walked through the campus, that included a residential section for housing students, I noticed that each building we entered had the same *view to the sky* as back at the inn where we were staying. I also noticed the number of times I saw basketball hoops and picture murals on building walls that depicted a player from the NBA. Kobe Bryant was prominent. Even more so was Yao Ming, the seven-foot six-inch national hero who was in the midst of his Hall of Fame career in the Association.

We entered a classroom in the middle of a lesson, and quietly moved to the rear of the room to observe. There were probably sixty-five to seventy students seated in rows, each with a stack of books for different subjects on their desktops. As the class time ended, the teacher gathered their belongings and headed off to another room or building. During the break time that followed, students left the room, too. Some played basketball. Others waved to us from outdoor balconies, and a few gathered around us to test their conversational English. I didn't know at the time that China is the largest English-speaking country in the world. Several minutes later, students were back in the room they had left, ready for the next lesson and subject from a different teacher.

We left the school around midday, and headed to a nearby mall to get something to eat. As we entered the large foyer of the mall, we noticed a large group of people about fifty feet away excitedly pointing upward to something. Of course, we had to find out what the commotion was. As we got closer, we saw a life-sized mannequin of Yao Ming. Not only was it huge, but it appeared to be alive in the stance it was taking. I couldn't resist taking of photo of me, 6'1, standing next to this 7'6 mannequin.

Following dinner that evening, we returned to the inn one last time to pack our bags before heading out to the airport for our flight to the last stop on our trip in Beijing. One of the things that surprised me on our flights within China was, by some, a complete disregard for "Please remain seated until the aircraft has come to a complete stop at the terminal." When we landed, literally wheels just touched the ground, there were multiple men standing up to get their overhead bags. Then they just stood there in the aisle. When it was time to disembark, I had to use my *low-post-elbow* to clear a way for myself and others.

It was almost midnight when our ground transportation pulled into the entrance for the Wangfujing Grand Hotel. I appreciated the ambiance of the centuries old inn, but I would be totally honest in saying it was good to be back in the city. Later that morning we'd be meeting up with the students—and two colleagues—from Newton who were attending at the JingShan School for the semester. Most of the seven students I knew from their time at Oak Hill, only a few years earlier. We toured the sprawling school campus before visiting in on a lesson-in-progress. The class size was smaller, yet still was well above that which we had in our respective buildings, back in Newton. That night, the school's Principal treated our group to dinner where I experienced and thoroughly enjoyed my first *hot pot*. The bok choy was new to me, and has since become one of the staple vegetables that I now buy. Yesterday.

Following a good night's sleep, I was up at eight and took advantage of the many choices offered to hotel guests at the breakfast bar. A few of my colleagues were doing likewise. After "good morning" and "seeing our students was such a thrill" comments back and forth, I learned that we had a field trip planned for us that included bike riding, and we would be leaving before ten. I'd been riding a bike since my dad warned me about going through potholes. Or riding out onto the runway at Kennedy Airport. Or flying at breakneck speed down the hill towards the intersection of Hillside Avenue. *This should be fun,* I thought. At the appointed time, we boarded a small bus that had room in the rear to hold several bicycles and a rack atop for others, for the seventy-five minute mostly highway ride outside of the city. Soon, we were looking out the windows at more and more countryside and small rural communities, when the bus pulled off the roadway. Along with ourselves, off came the bikes, out came our backpacks and there was a helmet for everyone. I felt like I was back at the Bowen School getting ready for a bike safety ride with Officer Cindy Webster. We'd been riding for about thirty minutes when I looked in the distance to clearly see The Great Wall of China.

"My goodness. I'm looking at one of the wonders-of-the-world."

We rode for another fifteen minutes as the massive structure came into a clearer view with each forward pedal that moved the chain on the sprockets below me. A quaint little restaurant appeared on the roadside where we would stop for lunch before beginning our ascent to the top of the wall. *Compared to Yellow Mountain, I got this,* I was hearing the voice in my head urging me on. Following lunch, we made a last *nature-stop* before walking up the mountainside for about thirty minutes to a section of the wall. Our guides knew of this spot. It was safe, secluded and parts of the section of the wall we'd be walking on were quite weathered. Without hesitation I followed the lead, occasionally stopping to look back and wait for the others. Unused firecrackers from the New Year's celebrations months before were scattered along the walkway. The kid in me kicked in and I couldn't resist picking up and tossing several (away from my colleagues) to set them off. When we got to the highest point, I experienced a sense of triumph in that moment just as I had when singing the *high*-C in choir. Or running the half-mile in high school. Or getting the call with the job offer of a principalship. Yesterday.

In the days ahead, we'd visit JingShan Park (where a group of women were immersed in Tai-Chi), The Forbidden City, and Tiananmen Square. Truly an experience of a lifetime, and one that offered a continuous flow of windows and mirrors throughout for me to fully appreciate each moment.

The trip home took us first to San Francisco for a short layover before the last leg of the journey to Boston. This time, the flight was completely full so there was only my middle seat to find comfort in for the five-hour flight. It was late Sunday night when we landed.

I was back at school on Monday morning. Had a great day. Arrived as usual at seven in the morning, got my day organized, had a cup of tea, checked in with folks around the building, greeted the students at the main entrance when they arrived, led the morning announcements and pledge of allegiance, when *BAM!* Hitting me like a ton of bricks was what I had heard described as *jetlag.* My mind was telling me that I had an uncontrollable urge and desire to go to sleep, right away. *Right away.* I told Doreen what was happening and that I was going home for the day. The last part of the morning rush hour was just about over, and I managed the twenty-minute ride safely home, where I slept for the rest of the day, and half of the next. There really is something called *jetlag.*

Yesterday.

TOMORROWS

I FOUND YA, YOU OLD AFRICAN

The British podcaster, author, and life coach, Jay Shetty, describes "flow" as *the moment that challenge meets skill.* When the new school year began in September of '08, "flow" would be an accurate descriptor for how our schoolhouse was operating and succeeding. The faculty and staff had returned to the friendly confines of the *six-day rotating schedule*, and the familiarity with F.O.H.G.Y.C.B in the building was one you could name and observe. This change was probably the most important for the adults in the building because it was evident that their collective voices had been heard and action taken.

Murals of famous people and their words representing a cross section of identities were appearing in different parts of the building.

The small faculty learning communities throughout the schoolhouse returned to examining student learning and reshaping the best outcomes. These same adult communities provided a seed for each grade level to include students in experiencing the ongoing flow with the creation of what came to be known as *community time* on each team in grades 6, 7 and 8.. Even some of the specialist teachers and student services providers joined with a team as well, and became a part of that community.

Returning to the rotating schedule realigned the daily operation of school and brought back, among other things, the Jeopardy-themed geography bee, a talent show, and a *pi* contest (as in 3.14). All were student favorites to try or watch their classmates in different roles. And the adults, too, had several "I didn't know you could do that" moments. For some, the five day schedule of the previous year had inhibited their participation.

John and I, much to our surprise, found additional places in the *old-now-new* schedule to share resources between our two buildings in areas such as world language and music.

We were continuing to go through a process of *rethinking middle school*, and I tried my best to remove the acronym B.R.I.M. from any notifications, conversations, and acknowledgements with my colleagues. However, the scheduling work and rethinking some curriculum under the umbrella of B.R.I.M. led to a wonderful opportunity that would turn out to be life changing for me.

Teachers 21, a local non-profit that provides professional instruction, coaching, and consulting to schools, was interested in finding out more of our work and its results, since our idea of rethinking middle school had first been shared through professional interactions with the organization a few years ago. Peg, herself a former middle school Principal, now working for the non-profit, reached out to us through Brenda. Peg had submitted an RFP (Request for Proposal) that had been accepted to present at the ASCD (Association for Curriculum Development) national conference to be held in Orlando the upcoming March. She wanted to know if any of us would like to be a part of the presentation at the conference. I did not hesitate to let it be known that I wanted to go and be a contributing part for the presentation.

Truthfully, I had already looked up the date previously because I knew that my sweetheart from high school, *from many yesterdays ago,* lived in the Orlando area. The story of how Gail and I landed back-to-together-again after over forty years is a yesterday that now has so many tomorrows to look forward to each day. Being in love provides a tangible flow I can carry with me.

Gail and I first shared the same space back in elementary school at P.S.160. I didn't use the word *met* because to do so would not be accurate. Her birthday is Christmas Day, and this put her in first grade when I was being introduced to my kindergarten teacher, Mrs. Wood. On the playground, if someone is not in your class, especially your kindergarten class, you probably didn't know who they were. Such was the case for us.

Gail has a childhood best friend, Bernice, who is also a favorite cousin of mine. Their home base in growing up together was in the 120th Avenue and Troutville Road area of St. Albans. My dad would often take me there when he went to visit Bernice's grandmother (Grandma) and grandfather (Uncle Ellis). A year ahead of me in high school, Bernice said to me more than once, "I've got someone I want you to meet." It wasn't too long after that conversation with my cousin that I first met Gail, right there at my cousin's home on Troutville Road. Both in our late teens, we dated and fell *hopelessly-in-love* over the months ahead. I never forgot her kiss. Gail was the first woman I'd fell in love with.

Fast forward almost thirty years, I ran into my cousin Bernice in 1997 in the most random of ways and coincidental circumstances. Hank, my son who was now sixteen, my then wife Robin, and I were on a *family reunion cruise* to Bermuda. That was a glorious yesterday, meeting a family who shared the same name and learning of the history of our name and family lineage. My cousin, David Van

Putten, spent several years of travel and research to paint an accurate story of the Van Puttens' in the Caribbean.

One day while there in the town of Hamilton, we stopped at a small *mom-and-pop* store to get some beverages. We made our selections and proceeded to one of the two cashier lines. Hank and Robin were on my left. I saw the other line move and turned my head to see if it was shorter.

"Bernice?" I said in disbelief.

"Henry Stafford (she calls me that to this day). Look at you!" She said in a distinct, native accent. I remember Bernice visiting the island during part of the summer months while we were both in high school and coming back with that *really cool* accent. After a few shrieks, hugs, and *I-can't-believe-this*, I introduced her to Robin and Hank, who stepped up to the cashier to pay for what we were purchasing and headed for the exit door to wait for me as my conversation with Bernice continued. Bernice asked me "So, have you heard from Gail?"

"The last time I saw Gail," I said, "her sister Audrey was seeing a guy who had a white speed boat and wanted to know if I wanted to go water skiing-about 1971"

Without hesitation, she took out a pen.

"Gimme that piece of paper on the counter. Here's her address and phone number. She'd enjoy hearing from you."

"Okay. Will do."

In the months and years that followed, I began keeping infrequent contact with Gail by sending her greetings on her birthday (which is Christmas Day), and then again on Mother's Day.

I was sitting in a Principal's meeting at the Education Center in March of 2003 when my phone rang. I took my phone and swiftly stepped out into the hallway to limit my intrusion in the meeting.

"Hank," it was Bernice on the other end. With a somber voice she said "Gail's husband died." My mind immediately started to go back to the bus accident and the trauma it brought.

Without going into a lot of detail, she described an industrial accident that he did not survive. "She might want to hear from you." I called to extend my condolences, and sent her and her children a condolence card

I continued keeping the infrequent, twice a year pattern of contacting Gail, until October of '08 when I called to tell her that I would be in Orlando in March for the convention.

"Okay. Give me a call when you get here." Was her peppy response. One of the many things that I appreciate about Gail is the lens of positivity and happiness through which she views the world and lives her life. Gail has been through a lot of personal loss in her life. Many of the *anniversary days* of loss are in March, which is when we got back together. She's got flow. She cooks with flow, she gardens with flow. She's taught me the value of choosing to be positive among the negative. It rubs off on me and I try to extend the same to others in any way. Being healthy and happy.

Some people come into your life for a reason or a season. And when that reason and season no longer exist, you take the learning along with you and can move on. Such was becoming the current state of my relationship with Robin. After more than thirty years, something had to change for me. I was no longer happy, and not feeling any flow in our lives together.

I'm sitting in the JetBlue terminal at JFK on March 14th, on my way to Orlando waiting for a connecting flight. My phone rings. It's Gail.

"Are you still coming?"

"Gail? I was going to call you once I got to Orlando."

"I can pick you up at the airport, if you need."

That'd be nice, I thought. "Sure." I gave her my flight number and expected time to be there.

"Okay, I'll see ya soon." Which she did and as the saying goes, *the rest is history.* It's been like the yesterdays just after high school.

Gail would come to see me in Boston a month later that spring. I did likewise in June by surprising her with a phone call from the front porch of her home in Florida. In May, I announced my intention to retire and with faith in the Lord, I took the jump to join Gail, the love of my life, in August. We live each day for the promise of the tomorrows each one brings to us.

We officially got married in 2015 and now enjoy the many blessings of our blended family.

"I found ya. You old African." I say to Gail, every once in a while.

LIVIN-THE-LIFE-I-LUV-&-LUVIN-THE-LIFE-I-LIV.

I have found retirement life to be great and everything about the *golden years* is yours to make. I give thanks most mornings that I no longer have to get up, get dressed, and deal with a two-way commute. Being with Gail is an unexpected part of these *golden years.* We go to the beach on the Atlantic side, with regularity. New Smyrna is our favorite. It's also been deemed *the shark bite capital of the world.* This doesn't deter us from spending a weekend at a resort there or anywhere throughout Florida. Go to beaches on the Gulf side. Take a three-day cruise to the Bahamas. Sleep in late. Spent a weekend at the home of her best friend, Linda, only an hour drive away. Rent a pontoon boat and spend a day on one of the state's beautiful lakes. Drive across the state to Tampa Bay Downs for a day of thoroughbred racing, stay for a night and then visit a winery on our return ride back home to Casselberry. Seminole County is about ten miles northeast of Orlando, which is in Orange County. Times were fabulous.

Something, though, was missing for me. I had an *itch* to teach and do the work of equity and inclusion that was gnawing at me. *You should be doing something more,* my inner voice was telling me. When I told Gail, she said that I should, "Scratch that itch," if I needed to.

In the spring of 2011, Valencia College, one of the top community colleges in the country, was advertising in the print and electronic media that the school needed Adjunct faculty. So, I applied for one of the many positions advertised, and was invited in for a job fair that the school would soon be holding.

The first person I spoke with at the fair told me that with my credentials I was a bit overqualified for the positions. I got the same response from the second person I spoke with. I'd not heard that before about myself from anyone, let alone twice in a row. But this person suggested that I speak with a woman named Kathleen, who had an leading role in implementing a course entitled Student Life Skills (SLS). She pointed me toward a desk where Kathleen was speaking with others. As with the first two, she immediately noticed and commented on my credentials. However, she felt that I would be a good fit and offered me a position to teach SLS two days a week on Valencia's East Campus. As our conversation ended, and I had received all the necessary information and filled out the initial paperwork, she said to me, "Have you met Rachel Allen?" Rachel was spearheading the Peace and Justice Initiative on campus, and Kathleen, also noticing my work in racial identity, felt that PJI could be another place for me to land at the college. How right she was.

I started teaching the SLS course in the fall of 2011. Each of my three sections brought a jolt of adrenaline when we'd meet on Tuesdays and Thursdays. I was massaging the *itch* I had and the interaction with college students was like a cherry on top, to complete my trip from elementary to middle to high school, and now at an institution of higher learning. Moreover, the age range of the students I interacted with extended beyond the traditional eighteen, nineteen, or twenty-year-olds to include adult learners who were returning to the classroom with a goal of making a career change.

SLS is a general education state required course that students had to take within their first fifteen credit hours of coursework. It was designed and guided by the six Ps: *preparation, personal connection, purpose, planning, place, and pathway.* Completing the course would assist the student in setting up a program of studies that would help each realize their long term academic and career goals. Initially, the burst of energy I experienced was carrying me on the crest of a wave that was unfamiliarly, *familiar.*

I hadn't forgotten, though, that Kathleen had directed me to seek out Rachel Allen and I did. We spoke for almost an hour in her East Campus office, where we exchanged stories about the work she was doing on campus, and what I had been doing before retiring. I started attending the gatherings of PJI where I learned about the practices of the Principles for How We Treat Each Other, the foundational principles of the on-campus organization. I soon found myself being offered the opportunity to co-facilitate a session about race (in the wake of the death of Trayvon Martin) for the Conversations in Justice Week, sponsored by PJI.

One weekend, a couple of years later, Gail and I were getting ready to head out on one of our frequent weekend adventures when she noticed that I was gathering papers and my computer to bring along.

"What are you doing?" She inquired.

"I've got papers that I have to correct this weekend."

"While we're at Linda's?" I could hear the consternation in her voice.

"Yeah", I sheepishly replied.

That certainly didn't go well. I was filling my time with tasks at the college that were taking away from retirement time. Time with family. It was a window and mirror into yesterday when I was teaching PE, directing a day camp, and coaching track and field, I had heard a similar voice call me out when my coaching began to extend through both Saturdays and into Sundays.

"You gotta change something, Hank." Gail insisted. "I thought you were retired! I didn't wait all these years to find you again, only to have you going back to what you were doing. THIS is an alternative universe you're living in now.!"

She was right. Although my Dean, Leonard, had made accommodations for me on my class schedule (Tuesday and Thursday, 10 AM to 2 PM), the volume of papers to read and correct for my three sections was not what I wanted to continue doing in retirement. So, beginning with the 2014 academic calendar, I informed my Dean that I'd no longer be teaching SLS (now reimagined and called the New Student Experience) and directed my energies to supporting the work of PJI. *No more correcting papers.*

The organization was growing, and this was a wave I wanted to ride. The Peace and Justice Institute was now extending out into the greater Orlando area and surrounding counties. PJI is guided by the mission of, "Making a difference by intentionally engaging in principles and practices that explore, advocate, and honor the dignity of self, others, and the earth." The foundation of PJI's work are the Principles for How We Treat Each Other. I'll say more about them in a bit.

A representative from the City of Orlando reached out to PJI after attending the Justice Week event in January, *Conversations on Race.* Their vision was to bring the institute's work to city employees and build capacity for the entire Orlando community. Two events that followed indicated the commitment that Orlando Mayor Buddy Dyer was willing to make.

The first was *Orlando Speaks.* These community events were held over a series of months in different district's throughout the city. Each event saw police officers from, the Chief to Patrol Officers, meet with citizens in guided discussion about their shared human experiences, in light of the current national events. Events that saw a series of unfortunate deaths of Black women and men at the hands of police officers. One commonality that came out of each of these gatherings was the desire to safely go home to family at the end of each day.

The second would be to provide a session—Conversations In Inclusiveness—as part of the hiring process for all new city employees. In the two hour session, the PJI Principles were highlighted to demonstrate what *inclusive excellence* is-the recognition that a community or institutions success is dependent on how well it values, engages and includes the rich **diversity** of its members. Still in place today as part of their onboarding process for new workers, this session has been completed by over three thousand employees, including the Mayor, Chief of Police and Fire, police officers, firefighters, first responders, City Council members, sanitation workers, traffic enforcement, and many other city employees.

I found room on my plate for a little more. Something that would not require correcting any papers. I submitted for consideration a course outline to the Teaching and Learning Academy (TLA) on campus. The TLA "assists tenure-track faculty develop a reflective approach to their teaching that is anchored in the tenets of action research." The program supports professors in their pursuit of achieving tenure at the college. I modeled my six-session hybrid course design (some face-to-face, some online) after the PD course I had taught for EMI while working in Newton. My submission was approved and accepted. *Authentic Conversations in Privilege, Racism and Academic Achievement* was added to the list of course offerings to faculty college wide, including the TLA. The only correction I'd be doing (as planned) was responding to guided online discussion comments that those enrolled would make each week. There were a few times when we went to the beach and while enjoying the sunshine, I'd have my computer handy and type out responses to the postings made. I'd have between eight to twelve professors enrolled in both the fall and spring semesters. If someone was to have asked me years ago what I envisioned this time of my life being like, what I was now doing wasn't far from my thinking in those yesterdays back then.

One fall semester about 2016 about three weeks into the course, one of the cohort members emailed me to say that he was not going to do the weekly reading and discussion assignment (completing the Implicit Association Test, IAT, and prompts) because, "I didn't know the course was about race."

I did that head scratching thing again because the word *racism* is in the course title and the first sentence in the syllabus reads, "The purpose of this course is to invite faculty participants to begin/continue to examine their professional and personal experiences using a lens of privilege and *racism*." I had to wonder if he had read the syllabus, just as we ask our students to do each semester. The professor went on to say that the prompts for the online discussion—one set for folks who identify racially as being in the global majority, and a similar set for those who identify racially as white—was not appropriate. He expressed that the assignment was going to further divide people and that the IAT was not a reliable predictor of identifying racial bias.

I told my colleague, Shari (then heading up the TLA), and I set up a meeting with the professor for later in the week that would last for almost ninety minutes. Because he was balking at completing the assignment, I first needed to make clear that his choice, not completing the assignment, would not allow him to earn any credit for the course. Completing all assignments was also in the syllabus.

I was aware of the history of the IAT (Harvard's Implicit Association Test), who the researchers were and the ongoing controversy about its use. "The Implicit Association Test (IAT) measures attitudes and beliefs that people may be unwilling or unable to report. The IAT may be especially interesting if it shows that you have an implicit attitude that you did not know about." There are over ten different assessments to measure bias one can complete. I'd completed the *Race IAT* twice. Initially, when I first began facilitating for EMI, teaching a course entitled Active Anti-Racism and Effective Classroom Practices, my results came back that I had a "moderate automatic preference for European Americans over African Americans". THAT was a surprise, yet informative for my further development.

Around 2017, I repeated the same IAT. This time my results indicated a "moderate automatic preference for African Americans over European Americans." Bias CAN be unlearned. Just like learning, it is a process.

One of the architects of the IAT, Claude Steele (author of *Whistling Vivaldi)*, visited Valencia for two days, meeting with students and faculty. He would acknowledge the controversy about the tools, reliability, and go on to say, "We have to begin somewhere."

So, I said to the professor who was balking to complete the assignment, "Do you know of another tool to measure racial bias that you'd like to use? If so, I'd welcome the opportunity to see it and for you to use it to finish this assignment."

Crickets.

Over the time of our conversation, I'd found out that this professor, a white man, identified as gay, was a republican who did not support the Trump administration, and was in a relationship with a Black man. I asked if he and his partner had ever had a conversation about racism.

"No. We don't talk about that."

I wasn't backing down on maintaining the integrity of my course, and he indicated that he couldn't continue if he had to complete the assignment. *No problem.* "I'll withdraw you from the course."

In the many yesterdays when doing the work of an anti-racist educator, I've had many challenges directed my way in class and through an email in teaching this course. In fact, I invite folks to *speak their truth* about their experiences with racism, knowing full well that each of us has a different story to tell about those experiences. Conflict leads to transformation. That was the first time that a cohort member had taken themselves out of the course work. From my balcony view, he used his *white privilege* to do so.

NOTHING CAN BE CHANGED UNTIL IT IS FACED. – JAMES BALDWIN

*T*alking and *learning* about racism is not a frequent conversation that has happened in the same way as, for example, conversations in math, science, or English. The conversation about racism is often based on limited experiences that offer monolithic or negative points of view, based on a deficit model about folks of the global majority.

The conversation about racism is not one that is just about the black and white dichotomy. To do so would make invisible the experiences of those who identify racially in other ways, such as Asian American, Native Hawaiian, Pacific Islander (AANHPI), Native and Indigenous, Hispanic/LatinX, bi/multi-racial or other ways folks choose to identify racially. It's also important to say that the conversation about racism is not an oppression Olympics. That is to say, "what about gender/sexuality/socio-economic status/ability/ageism?" Racism, as I have found, intersects with these and *many* other aspects of identity.

In the work I have done for thirty years of yesterdays, I've learned to view racism through a lens of a *system of advantage based on race*—a set of culturally acceptable beliefs that defend these advantages. And these systems are working as they were intended to do so; in support of some but working against and disenfranchising many others. Using this lens, I have learned that racism is expressed in three different ways: at the personal level, the cultural level, and the institutional level.

Examples of *Racism at the individual* level is when a person calls another a name, writes something on a wall, carries a tiki-torch while shouting racial epitaphs, calls the police about being threatened by a bird watcher or incurs violence on another George Floyd, Breyonna Taylor, Ahmad Aubery; this racism is clear to see. As Denzel Washington put it, "Racism hasn't changed, it's just being filmed."

In one of the sessions I co-facilitate, we ask the group to share a story of when they were either witness to, or on the receiving end of racism. One of the stories from yesterday that I shared happened when I was in college. I was traveling back to Boston from LaGuardia Airport on the Eastern Airlines Shuttle. The bargain fare of thirty-nine dollars one way was paid at the gate or once onboard. I was about nineteen or twenty, a six-foot Black man with a big afro. After paying my fare at the counter, two men dressed in suits quickly approached me and directed me away from the waiting area and toward a door that led to a back room. Almost simultaneously, I saw two other Black men about my age being escorted in the same direction. Inside the room, the short conversation with each of us went like this.

"Why did you buy a one-way ticket?"

"Are you carrying any weapons?"

"Can I search your hair?"

Examples of *Racism at the Cultural* level can be seen in the messages being sent about what it means to be "normal." Ibram Kendi writes, "Whoever creates the cultural standard usually puts themself at the top of the hierarchy."

For example, the push back against former NFL quarterback and current civil rights activist, Colin Kaepernick, for 'taking a knee' during the playing of the National Anthem. Or changing one's name to ensure being considered in the applicant pool for a position. Austin Channing-Brown writes about this very thing, the story of her name, in her book, *I'm Still Here*. The author describes a conversation about her name with her parents when she first learned about the systemic advantage her *masculine* sounding name afforded. It was an intersection of identity she was thankful for learning about.

Examples of *Racism at the institutional* level, such as government, criminal justice, real estate, education. and more, are historically, deeply entrenched. For example, the academic tracking that was part of my public-school education. The resistance by the white families in Jamaica Estates to our attending school there many yesterdays ago, remains with me today.

Michelle Alexander, in her book, *The New Jim Crow*, writes, "By the beginning of the 20th century, every state in the South had laws in place that disenfranchised blacks and discriminated against them in virtually every sphere of life: schools, churches, housing, jobs, restrooms, hotels, funeral homes, morgues and cemeteries." My parents, my grandparents and my great grandparents survived through those systemic disadvantages before and during the Jim Crow era. They found ways to thrive and to show and guide me on a path that I might be here today, and for the tomorrows still to come.

I often introduce myself to others as an *anti-racist* educator. I think that *who is racist* is not as important as *what are you doing* that is working to create anti-racist policies, practices, and procedures that push back against inequality. There are three givens that describe this work.

First, anti-racism is a verb. It's actionable. You can't stand idly by, disassociating yourself from the systemic advantage that is evident to you.

"If you are neutral in the face of oppression, you have chosen the side of the oppressor." - Desmond Tutu

Second, as I said, racism is not just about the black and white dichotomy. In this way, anti-racism casts a net of inclusion where all people, all voices, matter. For example, I use the app *Native Land* which allows me to know and share the name of the Indigenous Tribe on the land we are standing on in the PJI Academy for Teachers. Here in Orlando, this is the Timuka (tee-MOO-qua) Nation. Their peaceful history living as a community in this area can be traced back more than one-thousand years. That all changed for the worst in the early 16th century with the arrival of Ponce De Leon in what is now St. Augustine.

Third, anti-racism is not just about racism because of the many intersections that racism has with other aspects of identity such as gender, ability, nationality, just to name a few. Kimberly Crenshaw has done extensive research on the concept of intersectionality that examines where one individual experiences oppression from more than one systemic advantage. These intersections are windows and mirrors that create human connection.

A few years back, I became friends with a woman, Alma, from Mexico living here in the US as an "undocumented." We had met at a professional development weekend led by Lee Mun-Wah in Oakland. He is "an internationally recognized documentary filmmaker, and master diversity trainer." Throughout the weekend, I listening to her and others share their stories which added other perspectives for me to see through voices previously unheard by me. The interactions I've had with Alma since then have also highlighted my own privileges in ways I had not considered previously. Our conversations have created a *human* connection.

WHEN IT COMES TO RACISM, ARE YOU A NON-RACIST OR AN ANTIRACIST?

That's the question that I pose to everyone in my courses and during workshops. What is the action you are taking by speaking out, educating others, and getting involved in pushing back against the systemic racism that, in the words of my mentor and professional friend, Beverly Tatum, "is in the air we breathe." The Reverend, Doctor Martin Luther King Jr, speaks to the importance of taking action when he said, "In the end, we will not remember the words of our enemies, but the silence of our friends." In other words, there is no such thing as being a *passive anti-racist*.

I include the foundational work of PJI, The Principles for How We Treat Each Other, in my courses. Collectively, they create a powerful way to strengthen the culture of collaboration and trust in professional interactions. Applying the Principles for How We Treat Each Other brings the practice of making human connections into reality. These practices are:

1. **Create a hospitable and accountable community**. We all arrive in isolation and need the generosity of friendly

welcomes. Bring all of yourself to the work in this community. Welcome others to this place and this work and presume that you are welcomed as well. Hospitality is the essence of restoring community.

2. **Listen deeply**. Listen intently to what is said, listen to the feelings beneath the words. Strive to achieve a balance between listening and reflecting, speaking, and acting.

3. **Create an advice free zone**. Replace advice with curiosity as we work together for peace and justice. Each of us is here to discover our own truths. We are not here to *set someone else straight*, to "fix" what we perceive as broken in another member of the group.

4. **Practice asking honest and open questions**. A great question is ambiguous, personal, and provokes anxiety.

5. **Give space for unpopular answers**. Answer questions honestly, even if the answer seems unpopular. Be present to listen not debate, correct, or interpret.

6. **Respect silence**. Silence is a rare gift in our busy world. After someone has spoken, take time to reflect without immediately filling the space with words. This applies to the speaker as well–be comfortable leaving your words to resound in the silence, without refining or elaborating on what you have said.

7. **Suspend judgment**. Set aside your judgments. By creating a space between judgments and reactions, we can listen to the other, and to ourselves, more fully.

8. **Identify assumptions**. Our assumptions are usually invisible to us, yet they undergird our worldview. By identifying our assumptions, we can then set them aside and open our viewpoints to greater possibilities.

9. **Speak your truth**. You are invited to say what is in your heart, trusting that your voice will be heard, and your contribution respected. Own your truth by remembering to speak only for yourself. Using the first person "I" rather than "you" or "everyone" clearly communicates the personal nature of your expression.

10. **When things get difficult, turn to wonder.** If you find yourself disagreeing with another, becoming judgmental, or shutting down in defense, try turning to wonder: *"I wonder what brought her to this place?" "I wonder what my reaction teaches me?" "I wonder what he's feeling right now."*

11. **Practice slowing down**. Simply put, the speed of modern life can cause violent damage to the soul. By intentionally practicing slowing down, we strengthen our ability to extend nonviolence to others—and to ourselves.

12. **All voices have value.** Hold these moments when a person speaks as precious because these are the moments when a person is willing to stand for something, trust the group and offer something they see as valuable.

13. **Maintain confidentiality.** Create a safe space by respecting the confidential nature and content of discussions held in the group. Allow what is said in the group to remain there.

It was May of 2020 during the height of COVID. I signed into ZOOM as my colleagues and I were prepared and ready to greet the 20 or so virtual attendees to our annual PJI Academy for Teachers. I brought my computer into the light of our dining area, propped it up on a couple of books, and put on my headphones—the kind that fit at your temple on either side of your head but not in your ears.

I turned the brightness of the light up in the dining room.

After a couple of hours, I moved to the living room which was putting out more light as the sun moved from morning to afternoon.

This pattern of finding the correct lighting went on not just on that day, but all throughout the week as I co-facilitated multiple sessions from the "gallery" of ZOOM world.

During that weekend, as our team was debriefing online, my doorbell rang. I excused myself for the moment from the meeting and answered the door. On the porch, I found a package addressed to me. Not wanting to keep my colleagues waiting, I returned to the debriefing. But for some reason, my colleagues wanted me to open the package, so I did.

My colleagues had been watching me all week trying to adjust my light, and they also had noticed that I was constantly adjusting my headphones. I opened the package and to my surprise and delight I found a ring light, and a pair of Apple earbuds! I was beyond words of gratitude. My colleagues lived out Principle #1 - *create a hospitable and accountable community.*

In concert with my daily mindful meditation practice, these principles have allowed me to turn off my automatic response in any situation, personal or professional. By turning to wonder, they also test me each day to suspend judgment and challenge my assumptions about someone or something different. I've noticed that I listen to understand, not respond. Perhaps most importantly, I've learned the value of slowing down to enjoy the tomorrows arriving with each moment of each day.

FAMILY

When I was teaching the NSE (New Student Experience) at Valencia, an important part of the semester brought focus to one's purpose. What is it that gets you up each morning? What are you passionate about? What is your *ikigai*—the Japanese word that describes a sense of purpose for a person. Today, my *ikigai* is simply to be healthy and happy.

I've found ways to support my *ikigai* each day. This was one of the few positive outcomes of COVID. By practicing the PJI Principle #1, my PJI colleagues, Celine and Lianna, provided regular *online self-care sessions* for our community. "Given the times of unrest in which we are living, what are your self-care practices each day?" I found three that I continue to practice.

The first is spiritually. I get up each morning and give thanks for being awakened to see another day. I ask for forgiveness of my sins, both known and unknown, by word or deed. I test each of my senses to know that I'm alive and in the moment. I read daily verses from a childrens' bible book that is reminding me of what I learned during my time in the Grace Church Choir. I read from a book of daily writings by Iyanla Vanzant, *Daily Meditations for People of Color*, that will sometimes bring greater meaning to a day through its messages. Most days when I go outside, I kneel down on the grass, place my hand down and thank Mother Earth for all She has done for us, and ask forgiveness for all the harm we have done to Her.

The second practice I previously mentioned is my daily mindful meditation. I use an app and there are three speakers I listen to regularly—Tamara Levitt, Jeff Warren, and Jay Shetty. I've learned about impermanence and the importance of being present in each moment, bringing the best along and leaving the rest behind. Everything changes. I've learned about equanimity, finding in each moment what is here for me. Being able to move through discomfort and not be derailed by it is an important part of responding to the question, "Who am I?" I find that their messages during a guided meditation, individually or collectively, also often compliment the meaning of my day.

Third, I'm a model railroader. I have a four-by-eight tabletop at one end of our home where I have two trains running on two different ovals in opposite directions. Lots of detail that I keep adding on to. I spend parts of some days simply sitting and watching them go round, listening to the *clickety-clack* of the wheels on the track. I also like to go for three-to-four-mile walks three times a week in and around our neighborhood. Do some stretching. Yoga exercises, then soaking in the jacuzzi.

Spirituality. Mental and physical health. Having fun. My *ikigai*.

Gail and I have a blended family. They are all my greatest source of happiness. Our blended family includes four adult children. Jamal and Hank are my two biological sons. Deanna and Matthew are Gail's two biological children.

Jamal is married to Tammy. They live in New Bedford, MA. and have four adult children-Chanell, Zeke, Isis and Jamal Jr. Jamal works as a construction foreman and

Tammy's career has focused on assisting others navigate real estate law.

Hank III is married to Jean, and they reside in Norwood, MA. with their three daughters. Nylah, Emmah and our youngest grandchild Amelya is entering pre-school. My namesake is a real 'girl-dad'. His passion is poker. Whether it's a small group of friends or a large tournament, he is responsible in supporting his family. Jean is a full time instructional support staff person in an elementary school.

Deanna, currently a Physical Therapy Assistant (PTA) is taking courses and well on her way toward earning her Doctorate in Physical Therapy (DPT).

Matthew, who enlisted in the United States Marine Corps (USMC) right out of high school, has risen to the rank of Gunnery Sergeant. His soon-to-be-wife Shea, a retail executive director, and their son James, named for Matt's dad, live in San Diego. OORAH!

In the sessions about identity, diversity, equity and inclusion that I co-facilitate, I often take the opportunity to talk about them all in response to the prompt "choose an aspect of your identity that you are proud of." There's another question that follows right after; *what is an aspect of your identity that causes pain?* Let me tell you how this plays out for me when talking about my family.

I noticed a few years ago during one of these sessions about identity that a certain response of others was causing me a visceral physical response. It happened whenever a participant would talk about their mother and father. *Turn to wonder.* I decided to embrace the feelings and I began to include in my stories of the remembrances of my parents so many yesterdays ago, and include the truth that my mom did not live to see my high school graduation, and my dad did not live to see my college graduation. Amazingly, people in different cohorts started coming to me to share that they too had lost a parent during their early years of life. It created a human connection, a window and mirror for us to talk through the pain and proudly share about our parents.

About the same time, my son Hank III started to refer to me as "the family patriarch." That too, hit me hard as I was forced to confront in a realistic way, my own mortality, like I had not done before. I am realizing that I am well past the halfway point of my trip through the galaxies. I started to include *being a senior citizen* as an aspect of my identity that was painful to talk about, and again I've embraced this new part of my identity. When folks come up to me at break time or a session to share about their struggles with accepting their mortality, I consider it a blessing. Making a human connection.

When I speak proudly of our children, grandchildren, and great grandchild, another connection is made with other folks. Some are amazed that I can remember all their names, ages, and accomplishments to date. Others take the opportunity to proudly share about their grandchildren. I never for-go the chance to talk about ours.

BLESSED AND PROUD GRANDPARENTS

*C*hanell is the eldest living in Virginia Beach. After earning her advanced degree (Masters in Social Work) her career path has led her to the mental health field. After working as a clinical intern, she, took a leap of faith and opened her own practice as a to further serve the youth in her community. She's flourishing.

Zeke is a middle school English teacher and is living In New Bedford, MA. He has earned an advanced degree and has found a niche with an age that many feel is at the most challenging point of their young lives. He's prospering.

Isis is in her third year of medical school and lives in Rhode Island. She was named class *valedictorian* in high school, and earned a four-year scholarship to Tufts University. There were some initial moments of discomfort with her new classmates at the beginning of freshmen year that was centered around her name, Isis.

"Are you a terrorist? Do we have to worry about you bombing the dormitory?" Whether in jest or some kind of witty remark from these newcomers to her world, the unsettling micro-aggression comments allowed us all to remind her of the meaning of her name—*Isis is the goddess of fertility and love.* Her studies in med school are laser focused on the ob-gyn field.

Jamal Jr, is living in New Bedford at home with his parents, Jamal and Tammy. For the time being, he has chosen to go to work post-high school. Buying his first car, with cash, was a goal accomplished. He began as a hard worker in the retail field, and

is now employed by the City of New Bedford. He takes an occasional course or two to keep his options open.

Nylah has a wonderful free spirit and is a senior in high school. Emmah, who loves reading, is a sophomore in high school. And Amelya can't quite spell high school yet, at age three. The sisters live in Norwood, MA. with their parents, Hank and Jean.

Troy is entering the fifth grade. He's a math wiz!

James is six. He is a superstar in the making who seems to have an unquenchable desire to be *the best of the best*—something that he's learning from his dad, Matt,  who learned it from his dad James, who was tragically taken too soon.

Great granddaughter, Aleia, is seven-going-on-seventeen. Her personality makes you just want to squeeze and hug her every minute.

Each is what the late, great Maya Angelou calls, "a rainbow in someone else's cloud," for Gail and I in the tomorrows we have ahead.

VAN PUTTENS IN THE CARIBBEAN

"Which ship are you sailing on? We can meet at eleven o'clock and take you and your wife for lunch. As you come out, on your left is a sign that says *Aruba*. It's in front of a gas station. I'll meet you there."

I had never met, in person, my cousin Jackie Van Putten. We had recently connected over social media in a private group bearing our shared last name. Being in this group, I had something confirmed I had heard my dad and more recently my cousin, David, tell me about. There are Van Puttens in significant numbers throughout the Caribbean. I've learned that significant numbers also reside in the Netherlands.

Johannes Van Putten lived in Holland, the informal name for the Netherlands, in the early eighteenth century. One of his biological children was Jacob Van Putten, who traversed the Atlantic to St. Eustatius in the Dutch West Indies in the mid-century. Cousin David's research uncovered and verified several stories about his accumulated wealth, and what he was doing with a portion of it. The Dutch were not enamored with the British in the 1700s, and when The Revolutionary War (between the fledgling breakaway colonies and the British) became known, the Dutch provided support for the colonists as they pursued their freedom from The Crown. Jacob, himself of Dutch descent, for a time, was able to take advantage of this dispute by supplying arms and munitions to the colonists and continued to build his wealth. When he was discovered, the British took his wealth and exiled him to another island in the Caribbean.

As the page turned to a new century, one of Jacob's sons, John, took advantage of an enslaved African woman, who gave birth to a son named Louis, who is my great-great-great grandfather. It is an unfortunate truism of the times, taking advantage of enslaved African women, that gives me the melanin in my skin color. Some of my cousins today are very fair skinned, while others have a darker complexion than myself.

In the Netherlands (Holland), is a town named Putten. *Van* translates to from. I proudly say that my ancestors are from Putten.

I had been sharing my excitement with Gail for weeks leading up to our eight-day cruise. We'd be spending a day in Labadee, Haiti, Willemstad, Curacao, and Oranjestad, Aruba.

"Have you talked to your cousin?" She'd ask when we departed on a sunny Sunday in late February.

"Oh, yeah! I'm looking forward to meeting her. Got your yellow hat?" I sent a photo to my cousin Jackie, of Gail wearing a yellow hat.

"Where are we meeting her?" I showed her the message on my phone that Jackie sent to me. "Hope we don't have to walk far." When you reach a certain point in your life cycle, anticipating the distance and time by foot was an important consideration for us both.

We had breakfast, returned to our room to gather our things, and headed for the elevator to go down to the gangway and meet up with my cousin. The hazy sun and tropical breeze provided a backdrop and prelude for the day ahead. I looked for the sign, but noticed right away that there were two other ships berthed ahead of ours.

"I don't see the sign." I said aloud as we walked off the front of the ship. So, we started walking. When we reached the ship's aft, I saw about another hundred yards away the gas station sign. A few steps later the *Aruba* sign. And then I saw Jackie waving her arms like a ground crew person marshaling a plane to the jetway.

Along with another cousin, Kenneth, with the same surname, we gave warm greetings to each other and then got into his car for a memorable day. It was like having our own special tour led by family who made us both feel like family! We'd meet another cousin, Tony, who joined us for lunch and on our ride back to the ship some hours later, Jackie stopped at the home of another cousin, Dora, for a few minutes of human connection. It was a day that opened tomorrows for me to find out about and enjoy more about my family.

I hadn't seen my cousin, Lucy, since we were kids playing in the backyard at 35 North Clinton Street in Poughkeepsie, New York. This was the home where my mom grew up, and the place where she would marry my dad. So, it was a surprise to have her reach out—in 2020 through social media—and share that the band she played with was going to be in Daytona Beach for a weekend.

"Is that near you?'"

"Oh, yeah!" I excitedly responded. "Give me the place and showtimes and Gail and I will be there." Jazz is *good* music to hear and the group Lucy was with, the Bobby BlackHat Band, put out some *good* music when we went to hear them perform.

Lucy is the only living person I know from my mom's side of the family. Her dad, Aetius, who had a successful career as a scientist, was my first cousin, my mom's nephew. He was several years older than me. She is his daughter.

35 North Clinton Street was also the home where Granny and my grandfather, Charles Lawrence, whom I never met, had resided. Granny's maiden name was Oscafora Stradella Bolin. She was the tenth, of the eleven children of Abram Bolin and Alice Ann Lawrence. One of her brothers, Gaius C. Bolin, would in 1889 become the first Black graduate from the prestigious Williams College, located in Williamstown, MA. One of *his* children, Jane Bolin, would become the first African American woman judge in US history.

Lucy gave me a set of hand carved chess pieces that her dad made, along with some black and white photos of Granny, Grandfather, my mom, other aunts, friends and *one* where I see my dad!

These are the stories that I pay forward to my children, grandchildren, and great grandchild for their tomorrows, the times that I will not see.

GRATITUDE

May you be well.

May you know sincere love and learn how to give it in return.

May you find a blessing in joy, both yours and the joy of others.

May you remember to give thanks for all that you have.

May you be gracious and extend gratitude to others.

May you be free of anxiety and worry—*HAKUNA MATATA*.

May you bring a compassionate heart to offer from your yesterdays.

May you find peace in all of your tomorrows.

BIOGRAPHY OF HANK VAN PUTTEN

A native of Jamaica, New York, Hank Van Putten earned his B.S. in Education from Northeastern University, and a M. Ed. from Cambridge College. Hank's career of 35 years in the Newton Public Schools in Massachusetts began as an elementary physical education teacher, continued as a middle school physical education, and concluded with 12 years as an administrator, serving as a Middle School Assistant Principal, then an Elementary Principal and lastly a Middle School Principal, a role he held until his retirement in June, 2009.

Hank is an author, speaker and anti-racist educator who has received training from internationally recognized scholars including Dr. Peggy McIntosh, Dr. Beverly Tatum, Dr. Jonathan Saphier, and renowned diversity trainer Lee Mun Wah. His interests have focused on the impact of race on the academic success of African American students. To this end he has taught a graduate course for educators entitled "Active Anti-Racism and Effective

Classroom Practices for All Students," and the Foundation Course in the Graduate Program of Conflict Resolution and Peaceable Schools at Lesley University.

Hank has been an invited presenter and speaker on many occasions, including:

- A TED TALK entitled "When it comes to racism, are you a non or an anti?"
- END 2021 International Virtual Conference
- The Ted Bogert Show and Vanessa Elchols COLORBLIND podcasts Orlando, Florida.
- The Harvard Law School's "PASSING THE TORCH: The Past, Present and Future of Inter District School Desegregation".
- The ASCD National Convention.
- State Convention of the Florida African American Student Association.
- UNITY Village, Kansas City, UNITY Church, Melbourne., Florida.
- Concerned Citizens Network of Alexandria, Va., Alexandria Va. Police Department, First Responders and Office of Cultural Arts, and Voices for Virginia Children.
- The Black Brown and College Bound Conference.

Hank is currently a Diversity Equity and Inclusion Facilitator/Trainer for the Peace and Justice Institute in Orlando.

Greatest among Hank's blessings are his blended family with his wife Gail. Together, they have four children, ten grandchildren, and one great-grandchild.

www.ingramcontent.com/pod-product-compliance
Lightning Source LLC
Chambersburg PA
CBHW071739150726
47998CB00005B/1712